Advance Praise for *Newborns and New Moms*

'Dr Farah Adam Mukadam has written a useful guide for new mothers. By bringing together the wisdom of traditional practices, scientific data, real-life experiences and opinions, *Newborns and New Moms* prepares you for the most precious gift of your life: your baby!'

Dr Nirmala Krishnan, Founder of The 20's and Art to Connect

'A candid eye-opener, *Newborns and New Moms* provides an honest take on life after childbirth. Strongly recommended to all new mothers!'

Naiyya Saggi, Founder of Babychakra

NEW BORNS AND NEW MOMS

Dr Farah Adam Mukadam is a family physician from Bengaluru, India. She completed her MBBS from Kasturba Medical College, Manipal and holds a Diploma in Family Medicine. She is a mother of two kids, a six-year-old son and a three-year-old daughter. She is a consulting physician at Narayana Hrudalaya Multispecialty Clinic, Bengaluru and has a special interest in providing breastfeeding and postpartum support to new mothers. She has a YouTube channel called 'Momstein' where she often busts myths around contemporary medical aid.

Instagram @dr.farah_momstein

Facebook @dr.farahadam

NEW BORNS AND NEW MOMS

An Urban Indian Mother's Guide to Life after Childbirth

DR FARAH ADAM MUKADAM

PAN

First published in 2020 by Pan
an imprint of Pan Macmillan Publishing India Private Limited
707, Kailash Building
26, K. G. Marg, New Delhi – 110 001
www.panmacmillan.co.in

Pan Macmillan, The Smithson, 6 Briset Street, London EC1M 5NR,
Basingstoke and Oxford
Associated companies throughout the world
www.panmacmillan.com

ISBN 978-93-89109-62-7

5 7 9 8 6

Typeset in Scala by Manmohan Kumar
Printed and bound in India by Replika Press Pvt. Ltd.

MIX
Paper | Supporting responsible forestry
FSC™ C016779
FSC www.fsc.org

To my tone-deaf father, who had great faith in my singing skills. Your conviction in my endeavours has always kept me going.
May you rest in peace, Pappa.

CONTENTS

1

TAKING CARE OF THE NEW MOTHER

Being a mother is one of God's greatest blessings. It might be difficult to see how fortunate you are when you are going through endless diaper changes and struggling with engorged breasts and backache. But once the daunting first two months after delivery are over and you have adapted yourself to motherhood, you will begin to enjoy this journey with your new life partner: your child! There is a chance that you may relive your childhood through the eyes of your baby and truly appreciate this time. The first few years with your baby will be tiring, without a doubt, but it will be the golden period for you. No one is ever going to shower you with the abundant adoration with which your little one will. You will appreciate these little things in retrospect, as I do now. The cuddles and snuggles and the endless laughter over a simple peek-a-boo are what that make the life of a mother richer. The feeling of a connection with your baby, once you have mastered breastfeeding, compares to nothing else. In this book, I will take you through the ups and downs you will face as a new mother. But don't let the challenges bog you down. If you are expecting or planning a baby, or just had one, then you are reading the right book.

When I was pregnant, the idea of a human being coming out of me was just terrifying! I had not anticipated that the real hardships of a woman begin after the baby is born. Apart from all the physical and emotional problems that befall on us after delivery, we are also subjected to conflicting advice from our doctor, granny, mother-in-law, mom, other mothers and of course, the Internet. Should I cover my head at all times because my mother asked me to? Is the masseuse's massage actually any good or is it just breaking my bones? Should I pour oil on my baby's head? There are so many opinions out there but very little wisdom to be found.

In a typical Indian household that has welcomed a new baby, there is a huge change in the mother's daily life. She is massaged daily, served fresh food before everyone else, asked to stay indoors and not allowed 'head baths' at least for a couple of weeks. These instructions and restrictions have been a part of the wisdom passed down from one generation to another. They had kept new mothers hale and hearty. But now jump to the present day and you'll see today's superwomen juggling jobs, homes, babies and their sanity. They have no time for themselves and no one to guide them but the Internet. This cocktail is ruining their health. It is time they revisited old traditions to look into the logic behind some of them. In this chapter, I will throw light on the logic behind the wisdom passed down through generations hidden beneath technical jargon in scientific journals.

The Forty-day Confinement Period

The first six weeks are a critical period for a new mother's recovery, and she is confined to her room during this time. In Chinese culture, it is called sitting the month and in Hindi it is known as *chhilla*. All my patients have complained about this confinement period. After the first two weeks of sitting holed up in one room, a woman starts to lose her mind. There is a baby sucking at her breast pretty much 24x7, the milk and sweat makes her sticky, she is perpetually oily, her food is bland, and she hasn't felt fresh air on her body in weeks. I, for one, was dying to step out of this security prison that my home had become after my delivery. In fact, the forty-day sabbatical is so extreme in some cases that there was a woman who was not allowed to even talk to her husband in that period. She was literally sentenced to solitary confinement by her mother-in-law. Years later, when her friend had delivered, instead of congratulating her on the new baby, she ended up sobbing in front of her recalling how tormented she had felt during her confinement period.

There are plenty of parenting websites and blogs saying that you can take a stroll in the park two weeks after delivery to get some fresh air. Before I debunk the myth that *it is okay to step out before the forty days*, let me remind you that the country where this advice comes from has no paid maternity leave (the country is the Unites States). So, don't take advice from them regarding the confinement period!

New moms are often reluctant to comply with this advice because the explanations given by the *nanis* and *dadis* for the sabbatical are quite creative and not so scientific. They say things like you'll get affected by the evil eye (*nazar lagna*) or the cold air will enter your bones (*haddiyon main hawa utarna*). For want of logic in their justification, let's not discredit their suggestion just yet. Similar advice, and might I add, reasoning, are seen in every other culture that has been around for more than 1000 years (such as the Mediterranean, Chinese and Latina). And as for the Americans, they have a heritage that is barely 300 years old. So, who should we listen to?

We have at some point experienced that our immunity is much lower during pregnancy. We are more prone to colds and need way more rest to recuperate. It is because the developing foetus is a foreign body and the immune system has to mount a reaction against it to eliminate it. However, this is our little baby and the body knows that it must preserve it. While the embryo gets implanted, there are changes in the uterus that allow the pregnancy to progress unharmed by the body's immune attack. Your immunity is, in fact, lowered to favour the accommodation and development of the foetus. This state of lower immunity continues after delivery too. The process of birthing and shrinking of the uterus causes more stress to the body and a woman takes anywhere from three months to a year to completely get back to her pre-pregnancy immune levels.

One of my friends told me that she used to go to work daily and was thriving during her pregnancy. Apart from the occasional cold and heartburn, she never had any issue. She was confused about the hype around low immunity after delivery and wondered why she couldn't go out like she did while she was carrying.

I am glad she asked.

After the birth of the child, the body works overtime to repair and restore its normal self. Some women's bodies take the slow and steady path to recovery. While in others, the immune system which was suppressed during pregnancy takes a sharp U-turn bringing the body at the crossroads of suppressed immunity of pregnancy and the normal immunity of the non-pregnant state. This is known as the Immune Reactivation Syndrome. Each woman's body gets back on track differently, and you could be anywhere between the two extremes.

In Immune Reactivation Syndrome, the immunity follows a rather drastic recovery course and goes into overdrive. In order to protect your body's reactivity from going into a frenzy on coming in contact with every virus and bacteria, it is strongly advised that you sit it out in your room and be looked after. Taking a walk in the park daily is out of question. Maybe a short visit to the hospital for a check-up is okay. I hope that in the coming years, this important aspect of maternal care will come into the limelight and new mothers will get home visits rather than be asked to come to the hospital.

In my experience as a family physician, I have seen women disregard the confinement period and complain about recurring colds and knee pain even after their kids start going to school. Why does the cold virus so persistently affect them and why are their knees always paining? Most doctors tell them it's because they don't have enough Vitamin D and their calcium levels are low. (I have seen plenty of male patients working in IT firms who never step out in the sun and have very low Vitamin D levels. Yet, their knees are not crying for help! In fact, most of us urbanites are calcium and Vitamin D deficient. That seems to be the new normal.)

One of my patients complained about how she never felt well again after delivery. This woman was at the peak of her health in her pregnancy. She glowed, she worked, and she multitasked. Yet, delivering the baby seemed to have knocked the wind out of her sails. She felt that she never fully recovered from child birth even after her daughter's second birthday. If this woman was so functional in her low immunity state during pregnancy, why was she so deflated after her child was born? Yes, you guessed it. She went out every other day and did not stay at home protected.

Women who have not observed postpartum confinement did not see any medical reason in parenting books and websites to support the practice. They thought it was an unnecessary restriction passed down through generations. Maybe a by-product of restrictive patriarchy, they reasoned.

There was no scientific reason behind *bones catching a cold,* yet they complained of pain in their bones. Before I attempt to solve that mystery, I would like to introduce you to: autoimmune diseases.

An autoimmune disease is an illness in which the body's immune system attacks healthy cells. It runs a slow smouldering course and stealthily affects different organ systems before the person starts to show any symptoms. The patient has nagging aches and pains and respiratory complaints for the longest time and has to visit the hospital repeatedly in search of a diagnosis. More women than men are affected by autoimmune diseases. In fact, many women develop autoimmunity after delivery. Case reports have been documented of the postpartum development of different kinds of autoimmune disorders.

For instance, *Idiopathic Polymyositis* is a condition marked by inflammation and degeneration of skeletal muscles throughout the body. The affected patient has trouble swallowing and experiences weakness in lifting the head. Occasionally, the muscles ache and are painful to the touch. *Antiphospholipid Antibody Syndrome* and *Hemolytic Uremic Syndrome* both have effects on the blood. *Sarcoidosis* presents with swollen lymph nodes, skin patches and lung involvement. The effect on the lung results in symptoms of wheezing and cough. In fact, autoimmune disorders present usually with symptoms ranging from anything to everything. It can affect your blood, skin and bones, in particular. Autoimmune disorders are among the leading causes of death among young and middle-aged women in the United States. At least 85 per cent of patients with autoimmune disorders are females.

When I was in medical school and was having a discussion with my brother (also a doctor), he asked me, 'Why do you think women are more affected by autoimmune disorders? The disparity between the numbers of men affected versus women is enormous.' To which I smugly replied, 'Because we are our worst enemies.' He was amused by my tongue-in-cheek response and that was all that I had to offer at that time but now my view on it has changed.

The effects of improper care in the vulnerable state of immune reversal can partly explain the high prevalence of autoimmunity in the female population. The women who complain of vague aches and pains are either called psychos by their husbands and doctors, or receive sparse attention. I don't mean to be disrespectful to the doctor community, but this sounds a lot like what used to happen in the dark ages. A common diagnosis in those days was hysteria. A woman diagnosed with it had symptoms such as nervousness, fatigue, high libido, loss of appetite and 'tendency to cause trouble'. Hysteria was also called 'widow's disease' because it was seen in women after they got widowed. The 'wandering uterus' was blamed for it (hysteria derives its name from the root word 'hystera', meaning uterus). And the treatment was massage of the female genitals till the patient reached orgasm. In fact, vibrators were invented as a cure for hysteria because the doctors got tired of massaging so many patients! Simply put, after losing their husbands, they had no release for their sexual desires and that was driving them nuts, but back then they were seen as crazy troublemakers and some doctors even took the extreme step of surgically removing the uterus!

Just like the misunderstood hysteria patients of the past centuries, is today's modern woman who complains of vague aches and pains for years after her delivery. Bad knees, bad back, bad skin and feeling fatigued are the most common symptoms reported by these women. The doctor prescribes a long list of tests and the ailing patient returns with an empty purse without real proof of a disease. Years after tons of X-rays and blood tests, these women get diagnosed with autoimmune disease or the diagnosis remains a mystery because it is just chronic inflammation and not a full blown autoimmune disease. Meanwhile, when they undergo the sixth blood test in six months, they are called crazy behind their backs just like the women in the middle ages. Some things never change, do they?

So, what is actually happening in the female body with Immune Reactivation Syndrome? When the woman's immune system is reversing, her circulation is flooded with a different variety of white blood cells. The profile of the immune hormones produced by these cells also changes rather drastically. It has not been studied in detail in post-partum women but there is another disease that has been studied extensively. It is HIV.

HIV-AIDS is a disease which causes destruction of the body's immunity making the patient susceptible to deadly infections by simple viruses and bacteria. When therapy for HIV starts, the patient, instead of feeling better, ends up sustaining way more infections. Pathogens begin to spread to other organs. On initiation of HIV therapy, the body's immune system starts getting stronger and reverting from its weakened state. This violent aftereffect of the HIV therapy is the classical example of the Immune Reactivation Syndrome. For instance, tuberculosis which was limited to the lungs ends up spreading throughout the body, particularly the bones and lymph nodes.

The pregnant woman is in no way the same as an HIV patient. Pregnancy is immune suppression to support life whereas in HIV, infection is a mindless killing of the body's immunity by the virus. Recovery from pregnancy has a tumultuous effect on the woman's body but to a far lesser extent than what happens when a patient begins treatment against HIV.

Keeping a woman with lowered immunity in the familiar confines of home for a mandatory forty days makes a lot of sense. It is hard. I have been through it and was itching to go out, but I am glad I listened to my mother-in-law. It's like your body is turned inside out and anything and everything coming in contact with it has the potential to spark an exaggerated response. Innocuous viruses you would encounter in the outside world which wouldn't even cause a sneeze, have the capacity to sow the seeds of future reactivity to their harmful effects and long lasting inflammation. The disease could manifest years later as an autoimmune disorder. It is not always certain what triggers the initial immune attack in autoimmunity, but it is very clear that both the environment and genes play a role. Every disease is multifactorial. Men and young girls contracting autoimmune disease points to the fact that it is not only because of inadequate care in a woman who has just delivered but there can be other factors that come into play as well. Protection of a woman in the first forty days could be one of the steps towards preventing something as ignored as vague joint pains or perhaps even a full-fledged autoimmune diseases in the future. And as for the mothers who did step out during their confinement, please don't go into a frenzy saying you are doomed. We are mothers. We are way more resilient than we are given credit for.

Belly Binding

Belly binding is a routine practice in Indian culture. Usually an old cotton saree is used to wrap around the woman's belly from the ribs to the hips. These days the belly wraps that are commercially available are elastic ones and easier to use. Right after my caesareans, I would hold my belly with both hands and walk to the bathroom fearing my organs would come spilling out through my caesarean incision. It's very painful to walk after a C-section and these belly wraps work wonders in reducing the pressure of the sagging pooch on the stitches.

If belly binding is done with appropriate pressure, tolerable to the new mother, then it reduces postpartum blood loss as seen by higher haemoglobin levels in such patients. It also reduces pain in C-section mothers. Many women think that binding the belly as tightly as possible will give them a belly 'as flat as a pancake' in a matter of few weeks and help reclaim their lost pre-pregnancy bellies. Before you even think of going down that road, let's do a reality check.

1. Everything has been turned upside down in your body to house the baby. The only bone in your abdomen, the spine, was curved excessively to balance your body. Your entire weight bearing was out of whack. A decent amount of tolerable pressure by the elastic belt increases the abdominal pressure and helps in stabilizing your strained spine.
2. The relaxed ligaments (under the influence of the hormone relaxin) need support too. This practice helps in their realignment to the pre-pregnancy state.
3. The muscle group running straight down your abdomen, the one you call abs, has had more than its fair share of stress during pregnancy supporting the growing baby. It is prone to separation after delivery – a condition known as diastasis recti. Providing support for at least 8–10 hours a day will help keep the divided muscle together and help in better healing. The belly support works along the same principle as stitches do. The injured or cut open skin is provided close alignment by using sutures to create bridging of the damaged tissue. Healing is really

the body's job (and not that of the stitches). That's how belly binding works – it allows the muscles to be close together to heal properly.

4. The abdominal binder achieves immediate waist reduction as the soft, fleshy tissues are compressed, squeezed and redistributed above and below the waistline. Also, it holds the abdominal muscles in, at the right tension, and prevents them from becoming loose and expanding further.
5. The misguided people who advocate bouncing-back-in-no-time advise wearing tight elastic corsets, restrictive belly pressure and what not. This reminds me of the medieval times where women were forced into tight clothing in order to look petite. Post-delivery is not the time for torturing your body in the name of looking good. If you apply very high pressure externally on your belly, then you run the risk of uterus prolapse. In this condition, the uterus sinks out of the open cervix and vagina. The high pressure can also translate to pushing the stomach up through the diaphragm and can lead to life-long acid reflux.

How to belly bind:

1. A family member can wrap a saree around your belly starting a day or two after birth. C-section moms also need belly binding early on as it helps support the loose belly skin and avoids pressure on the stitches while walking. The mother should be the judge of how much pressure she wants in the first few days.

2. If you are on your own, then you can use the elastic binders available in maternity stores and online. Place the binder on the bed and lie on it. Wrap it around your waist and lower belly and secure it. The fit is snug if you wrap it lying down.
3. Always make sure the pressure is comfortable. Bind for 8–10 hours a day for the first month at least.
4. Belly binding should be accompanied by Kegels. Especially, after vaginal deliveries when the pelvic floor has been stretched out, the bind's pressure on the abdomen translates to more pressure downwards on the pelvic area. Kegels will restore strength and tone your muscles down there. It's pretty much the only exercise you have to engage in the first few weeks after delivery in addition to breastfeeding and short walks around the house. Clench your pelvic floor muscles and hold the pose for ten seconds and then relax for ten seconds. Do five repetitions in a set and do this exercise thrice a day.

Covering the Ears

I have seen many new mothers come for their post-delivery check-ups with tiny scarves tied over their heads. In some cultures, it is believed that foul air and evil spirits enter the new mother's body through the ears. My mother-in-law for one was a big believer in the practice of covering the mother's ears after delivery. She would warn me *thand lag jayegi* (you'll catch a cold). I complied for exactly three days only to remove the scarf when she was out of sight. That was a mistake. The grandma logic behind the practice might make you want to roll your eyes but there are valid scientific reasons that underpin this homegrown practice of ear covering.

New mothers love to blame their pregnancy problems on hormones, so let's go ahead and do it some more. The ear, nose and throat are affected by these pesky hormones so much that women are sniffling through the nine months. Water retention and lower immunity during pregnancy are also responsible for these coughs and colds. These episodes are frequent and annoying, but nothing some steam inhalation can't take care of. One important part affected by these changes is a tiny tube called the Eustachian Tube (ET) that connects your ear to your nose and maintains the pressure on either side of your eardrum. If all this sounds too technical then just think of the last time you were on a flight and how your ear had felt stuffy during descent. You held your nose and blew to pop your ear. It was this tube that allowed the air to pass to the blocked ear. The frequent nose inflammations through pregnancy cause malfunctioning of the ET.

With an already compromised ET function, a woman enters the labour room to bear down for her delivery. Anyone who has delivered normally knows how you have to take a deep breath and hold it and exert pressure down without letting air out of your mouth or nose. To get a clearer idea, the next time you visit the toilet to pass motion, just observe how you do it!

I came across the case of a perfectly healthy woman who had an ear bleed right after her delivery. It came as a rather surprising twist to an uneventful labour. This otherwise fit pregnant woman's water-logged ET wasn't very adept at maintaining her ear pressure. The downward pressure she exerted with every arduous push increased the pressure in her head too. This force caused her ear drum to bulge and rupture causing the ear to bleed. If all this sounds too horrifying, then don't worry. The story has a happy ending. By her 6th-week check-up, the minute hole in her eardrum had healed on its own and she could hear just fine.

One does not particularly require antibiotics to recover from such a scenario. Usually eardrum perforations follow a middle ear infection and a high spiking fever. A perforation due to labour is because of excess pressure built up in the already weak ear without an actual infection. Covering your ears will provide the protection you need to prevent bacteria from entering your middle ear. Antibiotics are not really necessary but if you are one to rely on modern medicine for all your woes, you are covered in the ear department too. Your doctor would have prescribed a dose of antibiotics to keep your stitches infection-free.

Other reasons why a postpartum woman should cover her ears:

1. While bearing down during labour, the woman has to clench her jaws and apply pressure. This abnormal

pressure can cause damage to the joint in the front of your ear at which you can feel movement while opening and shutting your mouth. A patient with this injury is advised to cover his/her ears as even a gentle draft of cold air entering the ear canal can cause a painful spasm in the lower jaw muscles.

2. Every pregnancy is accompanied by hormonal changes which predispose a mother to a diabetes-like state with high blood glucose levels so that the baby always has ample fuel supply. Some women develop a pregnancy induced diabetes because of these changes which is called Gestational Diabetes Mellitus (GDM). Right after delivery, the blood sugars of the GDM patient go completely out of control only to settle six weeks later. Monitoring of blood sugar is not done at this time as reversal of the diabetes is occurring in the body and the test results could be misleading. The spiking blood glucose in this period makes the patient's ear canal susceptible to a nasty infection by a specific bacterium called *Pseudomonas*. So, cover up to protect your ears from this baddie!
3. Delivery reduces the overall weight of the woman by about 6-7 kgs (baby's weight + placenta + fluid). This sudden drop in the weight and water content of the body shifts the centre of gravity of the new mother. These changes disturb the delicate balance system of the body called the vestibular system which is located in the deeper parts of the ear.

As doctors, we know that pregnancy is a stressor to the inner ear of the woman as we get a lot of complaints of reversible hearing loss caused due to hormonal changes. Protecting the ears is imperative as a draft of cold air from the fan or even warm air could predispose the mother to spells of fainting or a sense of loss of balance.

Head Baths

Washing one's hair after having a baby is banned in most Indian households for the first six weeks. The new mother's usual bath is with neem leaves boiled in water poured only over the body. She is told that 'head bath' will lead to headache and dizziness. The poor woman feels like one deflated *puri* with oil dripping from her hair all the time. All she wants to do is kick out the masseuse, block out her bossy mother and stand soaking under the shower.

What does science have to say about this restriction? True to form, science calls this ancient wisdom a whole lot of rubbish.

With all the changes manifesting in a woman's ear, you are required to exercise caution just like any patient with ear problems. The moisture that gets left behind in the outer ear canal due to frequent hair washing can be a breeding ground for many bacteria. Exposure of the ear canal to hot or cold water temperatures could cause dizziness (so be sure to leave the bathroom door unlocked to get help in case of an emergency). If you have had an ear drum perforation due to pressure from the labour then you need to make sure that water does not enter your ear.

If you have had a normal delivery, then do give the 'head bath' a miss for the first couple of days. And the days you do decide to wash your hair, be sure to insert a cotton ball gently to cover your ear opening and smear some petroleum jelly around it to block water from entering your ear. (Don't insert the cotton ball too deep). Use warm water for your bath.

I have come across women on online forums asking if they can go into the jacuzzi after their delivery. The jacuzzi will send jets of water with high pressure all over. Your cervix is still dilated, and your uterus is empty. Don't force water into all that open space in your body but on the other hand, a Sitz bath would be great for you. It is routinely prescribed to patients with stitches in their vaginal region. Sit in a tub of warm water with some antiseptic in it. The warmth increases blood circulation in the perineum (the area between the anus and vagina) and promotes quicker healing. It is also going to help you with the genital soreness and prevent infections.

Proper vaginal care is important for mothers after normal and caesarean deliveries. Do not use menstrual cups or tampons. Since the cervix is open, chances of infection are high if a cup or tampon is inserted. Always opt for sanitary pads. Remove your pad by peeling it off from front to back (so that faecal bacteria is not carried to the vagina and urethra). For the same reason, always wash yourselves from front to back after passing motions.

Steer clear of intimate washes as they disturb the balance of healthy bacteria present in the vagina.

Massage

However, we have gotten ahead of ourselves. Before the bath comes the *maalish* or massage. In India, after every delivery, a *maalishwali* or masseuse is hired for a minimum of six weeks. The daily massage is regarded as one of the fundamental rights of a new mother. And here's why it is a valued aspect of post-delivery care:

1. During normal labour, the muscles of the mother become sore due to the excessive pushing and labouring. I wouldn't be wrong when I say that normal labour is one hell of an exercise. The trauma of delivering a seven pounder deserves top notch post-delivery care and there is nothing better than a deep massage to relieve the mother's tired muscles.
2. In addition, the mother's recovering immune system is flooded with inflammatory substances to recover from the stress of pregnancy. Massaging the muscles reduces production of these toxic substances and helps to bring the hyperactive immune system of a new mother back on track.

Aside from the immediate effects on muscle relaxation, the body's metabolism also stands to benefit from the deep pressure application. The massage is done with so much pressure that the woman is often exhausted by the end of it. So why are those *maalishwalis* adamant on crushing our bones? Well here too, our traditional wisdom doesn't fail to deliver.

During pregnancy, oestrogen and progesterone levels peak as the placenta pumps these hormones into your blood. Oestrogen is the feminizing hormone which gives you perkier breasts, rounder hips, glowing skin and lustrous hair. It surely sounds like a beauty product, but oestrogen is just prepping your body for housing a baby. Progesterone on the other hand, maintains the pregnancy, looks after the baby in your womb and stops milk from being produced till you have delivered (as that would be a precious waste of resources).

Oestrogen and progesterone are no longer required in such high quantities after delivery. Thanks to these hormones, you had been stocking fat during pregnancy for future use. After delivery, in a span of a few hours, the body must change gears from baby making and fat storing to baby rearing and milk making. This means:

1. To provide nourishment to the mother's worn out body post-delivery as well as to feed the baby, more effective fat usage must restart. Thyroid hormone, the fat burning hormone, is opposed by oestrogen, the fat storing hormone, throughout pregnancy. (That is why your doctor had increased the dose of your thyroid tablet

during pregnancy.) Once oestrogen exits the body, thyroid is free to gear up the metabolism of the mother.

2. The sudden fall in progesterone after the delivery allows the milk producing hormone, Prolactin, to act upon the breasts.

The excess oestrogen and progesterone in the body enter the cells passively from the blood and get accumulated in all cells, especially the fat stores. The liver and intestines are in a weakened state after delivery and fail to entirely control and eliminate this hormone flood. In a sense, the liver is overloaded by this hormone and is having a tough time excreting it from the body. This is where the skin can come to the body's rescue. A rigorous massage squeezes the hormones out of the cells into the blood and out of the body through the skin. Which brings me to the next aspect of maternity care: the *ubtan* (beauty paste) and hot water bath.

The *Ubtan* and Hot Water Bath

The *ubtan*, used to bathe the mother as well as the baby in the first forty days, is a homemade mixture of gram flour (*besan*) and turmeric. The gram is a cousin of the overly-glorified hyper-marketed soy. Not only are we all lapping up soy milk and soy chunks as the absolute and at times only source of protein, but we have been slathering its advertised goodness all over our bodies too. If you take a look at the ingredients of the priciest of soaps, you'll be sure to find soy. So, let's give its humble relative, the *besan*, a fair chance to justify its place in skincare too.

The new mother's blood stream is flooding with oestrogen from all that has been squeezed out of her cells because of the deep pressure applied during the massage (by the process of diffusion). Excess oestrogen is excreted via the skin pores facilitated by the deep massage (since our skin is partially permeable to oil and chemicals). The ubtan massage increases blood flow to the skin enabling oestrogen excretion via skin and the hot water dissolves it and washes it off. The sooner the fat storing hormone, oestrogen, leaves your body the leaner you will get. Doesn't that sound good? I thought so too! What makes it even better is that the good fatty acids from the coconut or sesame oil that was used for your massage will get absorbed into your circulation and promote more efficient fat burning.

Another advantage of application of ubtan is that it makes your complexion clearer and reduces pregnancy related patchiness. Unwanted body hair growth too stands to be eliminated from this ubtan regimen. So be sure to scrub it well on your arms, legs and armpits for skin more flawless than the one you were blessed with.

How to make ubtan:

Depending on your requirements, take few tablespoons of gram flour. Add a pinch of turmeric for every two tablespoons of gram flour. Make a thick paste in water and use it for application on your face and body.

2

THE NEW MOTHER'S DIET

Before I talk about eating well after delivery, I need to dispel one simple myth. Diet means something you eat, not starving in the pursuit of losing weight! So, a diet for a post-partum woman needs to be light, yet rich in proteins, fats and carbohydrates and miles away from words such as keto and green tea. I stand firmly against replacing carbs with fats and cringe when people throw around silly phrases such as 'good cholesterol' and 'bad cholesterol'. And as a doctor, I have to hear my patients ask me all the time about their 'bad' cholesterol. Cholesterol isn't bad. And neither is any other nutrient. When cholesterol was shunned worldwide by cardiologists, what soon followed was the boycott of egg yolk. Health nuts from around the world united and got behind the private protest against the deadly food that was the egg yolk. My husband was one of those health nuts and had an anti-yolk stance when I married him. I wasn't successful in getting him back to the whole-egg faith, but I didn't allow the ridiculousness of eating only egg whites in my house. All eggs are served whole.

Egg yolk is the life bearing part of an egg. The egg white or albumin supports the egg yolk. Some of the nutrients you are throwing away while gorging on egg whites alone:

1. *Vitamin D*: Egg yolk is one of the few food sources of Vitamin D. Our body gets most of its Vitamin D supply from the sun. And if you have been raised a true blue Indian, you consider the sun your enemy and avoid tanning as much as you can! So, get your Vitamin D from a sunny-side-up without the tan.
2. *Vitamin B complex and Vitamin K*: These nutrients run the machinery of optimum energy usage in your body, give you great skin and hair, promote gut and blood health. If you shy away from fruits and vegetables, then egg yolk can make up for it.
3. *Vitamin A*: Great for eyesight.
4. *Choline*: This nutrient is necessary for nerves and brain, especially for little kids. Many malt-based health drinks claim to be choline-enriched. The shameless ads for these processed diabetes-inducing drinks boast about how you are helping your child become brainier. Save your child from loading up on that junk in the name of a higher IQ. They are high in sugar and sodium and could make your child prone to obesity and diabetes in the long run. Toss the mug and reach out for the egg yolk.
5. *Iron and Folate*: Important for blood cell production in the body. Egg is a rich source of protein, so your blood cell production gets the complete raw material from eggs.

6. The egg yolk has an excellent fatty acid profile as well. It is a great source of Omega-3 fatty acids.

The big secret about cholesterol that most websites, books and nutrition 'experts' fail to inform you about is that whether you eat cholesterol or not, the liver will produce cholesterol in the body. If the supply from food sources is more, the liver will compensate by reducing its own production. So why exactly is the liver adamant on pumping cholesterol into your body? Because it is one of the most important molecules for the human species. It is the molecule which makes the outer coating, that is, the cell membrane of every cell in your body.

In fact, one of the most disturbing side effects of cholesterol-lowering drugs was memory loss seen in people as young as thirty-five! About a quarter of your body's cholesterol is found in your brain. The complex branching brain cells that help you think and remember stuff are tampered with when you pop a cholesterol-lowering drug. Even hormones in your body such as oestrogen (the feminine hormone), testosterone (the masculine hormone), progesterone (the pregnancy hormone) and glucocorticoids (the stress hormones) are all derived from cholesterol.

Cholesterol is to the body what the brick is to a building. Every cell membrane is made of cholesterol. It is produced by the liver regardless of what you eat, and the body knows best how much to manufacture. Artificial reduction by medicines is like throwing a spanner in the works of the cholesterol-manufacturing liver. It's a single-track minded approach as though the body is a heart and nothing else (as cardiologists seem to view it).

Now if you ask me for a scientific guideline for the number of eggs you can consume in a day or a week, then the message I am trying to convey is just not hitting the mark. What you need to understand is that there is no lucky number of eggs to be eaten to be in the prime of health. Swapping oils for fancy gourmet imports is not the mantra either. In fact, the West went berserk with the fish oil craze. The Inuits of Greenland (who are popularly called eskimos) consume a diet laden with fat. Yet they had a very low prevalence of heart ailments. The link between fat consumption and heart attacks was in a manner openly challenged by these people's diet. On scientific probing it was found that fish was an amazing source of fat and the high Omega-3 content in fish was protective to the heart. You can imagine what happened next. The world scurried to load their bodies with fish oil capsules. And just like that the fish supply of the world's oceans was not enough for the insatiable appetite of the starving dieters. It is estimated that by the year 2048, the world's sea water fish supply will be depleted because of this unbalanced dietary craze.

This dieting duffery needs to end. Don't deem everything you ate as a kid, which was freshly cooked and served with love, as inferior to what the westerners or the skinny one eats. Eat in moderation whatever your tradition serves on your plate. Even non-vegetarian food if you wish. Going vegan or paleo, swinging between low fat and high fat and banning yolk or gluten solves nothing. It is just adding to your woes by stressing your brain with conflicting information and your body with fluctuating diets. Don't skimp on oil but don't binge on oily food either. Tread the middle path. Don't swear off carbs and neither should you splurge on proteins in the name of muscle building. Too much protein will become converted to stored fat as will too much fat and carbohydrate. And if there is anything you need to swear off to be healthy, it is pre-packaged food which are often laden with trans fats. And that is the stuff that is clogging arteries and attacking hearts. Not cholesterol. Not fat. Not carbs. Not gluten.

In short, you can eat the egg and have the yolk, too.

Eating Right After Delivery

Ashima was a docile woman who lived happily with her mother-in-law, daughter and husband. When she was pregnant with her second child, close to her due date, one of her husband's aunts came over to care for the household. The aunt had a heart of gold and a big guffawing laugh. She had come hauling a sack of jowar *atta* and custard apples from her hometown to feed the new mother.

After her delivery, breakfast for Ashima was a decent enough affair. *Dosas*, *idlis*, *paranthas*, *khichdi* or *poha* was the usual menu but she was not as lucky when it came to lunch and dinner. To Ashima's horror, the aunt had not only brought a truck load of custard apples for them but also a blanket ban on virtually every food item under the sun. For the next one month, Ashima was fed a diet of pretty much only tomatoes and cauliflower with rice and hot jowar *rotis* (the aunt was a roti expert). She would say the baby will get green stools if the mother ate green leafy vegetables. Ashima wasn't allowed eggs either. The aunt reasoned that the kid would get jaundice (yellowing of the eyes) because of the egg yolk. Ridge gourd was also off limits because that too is considered a cold food. Brinjals and potatoes were said to make the baby colicky. No *daal* (pulses/lentils) were permitted in her diet. She was denied guavas and oranges because according to the aunt they caused seizures in children. Over the next few weeks, every fruit was crossed off the list as too cold, too gassy or too whatever. One glaring anomaly was that these cauliflower vigilantes paid scant attention to their own diet and health. Both the aunt and mother-in-law were diabetics. They were scared of even one sugar crystal falling into their teacups and had totally shunned rice but they would binge on *sitaphal* (custard apple) and poured the fruit's sugar into their bloodstream like there was no tomorrow.

All the dietary restrictions were driving Ashima up the wall and her difficult post-delivery recovery was also taking a toll on her. The aunt who came to look after her was good natured but her ignorant ways were beginning to cause unsalvageable harm to poor Ashima. All the iron, vitamins and other micronutrients packed in fruits and green vegetables were denied to her. Her animal and plant protein intake was curbed, and her only sources of protein were rice, roti and milk. The protein profile in rice and roti is completed only by the accompanying daals and curries. *Methi laddoo*s and *panjeri* (a dry mix of jaggery, dates, dry fruits and coconut fried in *ghee*) should be a staple of every woman's diet after delivery but Ashima did not consume that either. She did not like dry fruits, so not eating those wondrous foods was Ashima's own doing.

Fast forward to four and a half months. Ashima got a terrible throat infection and was running a very high fever. After four days of suffering, she was started on antibiotics. By the seventh day, Ashima was beginning to have trouble breathing and felt a tightness around her chest. She was fatigued by the fever, a hacking cough and the breastfeeding. She had contracted pneumonia and had to be admitted to a hospital immediately. Her son, a little over four months, was abruptly separated from her and the *Dadi* had to take care of him. He was actually a good baby and took to the milk bottle offered to him rather keenly. Ashima diligently pumped in the hospital to keep up her milk supply but could not give her son the expressed milk because she was on a cocktail of antibiotics to fight the pneumonia.

In Ashima's case, her immunity had taken a beating because of all the food restrictions imposed on her. Her diet should have been abounding in proteins, fats and all essential micronutrients. Vitamin C found in the citrus fruits is important for body repair. The collagen produced by the body to heal the cut-up layers of the abdomen is supported by Vitamin C and zinc present in fresh produce. As a caesarean patient that was of utmost importance for her recovery. Virtually no vegetable and fruit were given to her besides cauliflower. The essential fats present in nuts, dates and coconut, which was in her panjeri, were not eaten (because Ashima had refused).

There is a lot of free advice being fed to a new mother. So many food items are off limits and so few on. General guidelines to be followed while choosing a diet for the new mother should be:

1. *It should be made according to the mother's likes and dislikes*:
   Many mothers will refuse the stuff extremely good for their health. They will need to be cajoled into eating the good-but-not-tasty stuff. But if the new mother complies with having the dry fruit rich laddoo that she dislikes, then do respect her wishes and cook her favourite curry for lunch. Just like we take care of our children's wishes while cooking for them but use innovative ways to smuggle greens into kids' dishes, a postpartum woman's needs and wants both need to be respected. If she is happy, then her nutrient absorption and assimilation will be better.

2. *Keep it simple and light: An ode to the single mother*
   While cooking for a new mother, try to maximize on nutrient profile along with the flavour profile. A friend of mine had to get on by herself after her second delivery because she lived abroad. She had to take care of her

newborn, her one-year old son, feed a lazy husband as well as nourish herself. She hired a maid to help out with the cutting of veggies and making rotis. She would cook easy and quick one-pot meals which were lightly flavoured and had a lot of nutrition. One of her favourite go-to recipes was chicken stew. She would saute garlic in hot oil followed by chicken, carrots, spinach and green beans. After seasoning with salt and pepper, she would add water and let it cook in a pressure cooker till the chicken was done. That would make for a great soupy stew in which she would soak her wheat rotis (a practice called *roti choorna*) and eat as her meals. It was simple, and she did rather well for herself on such a diet. So, for mommies who are going to be flying solo, keep a list of easy-to-cook (non-spicy) recipes ready during your pregnancy. Most mothers will back me up here when I say that the hardest part about cooking is deciding what to cook! With this pre-made list, your husband or you can whip out a dish in no time.

You can also prep for your post-delivery meals right in your third trimester. A simple preparation would be to make curry masala and stock it. Opt for a simple gravy base that can work for many Indian dishes. One such basic recipe would be: Fry onions till they turn golden, add ginger–garlic paste and saute for a minute. Add pureed tomatoes and let the mixture cook till the oil separates. When the curry mix cools, add to ice cube trays to freeze. Once frozen, remove the masala cubes, stock in a container and store in the freezer compartment. Whenever you have to cook, you can get a dish out in no time. Just add 2-3 cubes of curry masala, add salt and dry spices (minimize red chilli powder and avoid green chillis) and then the vegetable or dal. You can stock any gravy base this way. It is a much better alternative than store-bought ready mixes. Another preparation you can do is deep fry onions and refrigerate the caramelized onions. It can be used for quick *tadka*s and gravy bases.

To ease your digestion and gas issues (new mothers are highly flatulent after delivery), stock a mixture of equal proportions of carom (*ajwain*) seeds, fenugreek (*methi*) seeds, fennel (*saunf*) seeds and nigella (*kalonji*) seeds in a small air-tight container. You can have one teaspoon of this mix as a digestive after your meals. It will ease the bloating and improve digestion. As a bonus, the fennel aids in milk production and nigella helps with immunity.

Breakfast can be simple too. You could keep a stock of dosa batter ready for yourself. The aim of all these food suggestions is to make mealtimes a simple and nutritious affair for you. Store-bought batter is not a bad alternative if you are pressed for time. But remember it is super easy to make dosa batter and it can last you for three to four days easily. And homemade is always better and more nutritious. You could have dosa with fried eggs for a filling breakfast. All this preparation should not only reduce your efforts during postpartum healing – if you are handling everything alone – but also save you time spent planning meals. I would recommend staying away from ready-to-serve breakfast cereal. But do keep a stock of your favourite breakfast cereal for particularly difficult days when all you care about is a full stomach and not so much about top quality nutrition.

While you are busy freezing everything in your pregnancy, one great tip would be to cook double the quantity in your last trimester and stock one half in labelled containers in the freezer. That way you won't have to go out of the way and put in extra hours and effort to make your stock of meals.

Also, please ignore the husband the first forty days. Don't bother with packing his tiffin or making him hot breakfast. Just worry about yourself and your baby. If all goes well, you will be decently settled by the end of the first month. Then you can start taking care of the big baby that your husband can be.

3. *Sourcing your food: Frozen versus Fresh*

No one's nutritional requirements compare to that of a woman just after delivery. Her body needs iron, calcium, vitamins and other minerals in abundance to repair her worn-out insides. The new baby is sucking out her nutrient reserves through her milk and a mother's body is such that it will sacrifice the strength of its bones to nurture her child. Her iron stores had been compromised by pregnancy and they take a further hit once she starts breastfeeding. That does not mean she should not breastfeed to conserve her resources. It just means that she must eat smartly to optimize the resource usage for her health and that of her baby.

My heart really goes out to mothers who have to take care of themselves right after delivery and have no one to fall back on. The mother has to look after the cooking, run errands and get groceries, while handling a newborn. Grocery shopping is a huge task for a mother struggling to find her footing in motherhood. Online portals delivering supplies to your doorstep are perhaps the biggest blessing in today's fast-paced world but while shopping for fruits and vegetables, where does one draw the line between processed and preserved foods? Are frozen foods devoid of nutrients as many fresh food enthusiasts blame and claim?

No, not really.

Fresh food isn't always a harbinger of pure goodness. For fresh produce to be sold in the market, it needs to be plucked when raw. This means that the produce had not reached its peak nutritional quality at the time of harvest. And the journey from there is only downhill. The produce is packed in cargo trucks or ships to be transported to the city or even another country for sale in the retail market. That takes a few days at least and in those passing days, the nutritional content of the food also diminishes. The produce then sits on the shelves of the grocery store waiting to be picked by you. After which it is not consumed immediately but instead stocked in the refrigerator or on your counter top before it finds its way to your plate. During this whole journey, the fruits or vegetables lose close to half their nutritional content. Frozen foods, on the other hand, are picked or plucked after they are ripe, at the peak of their nutrient concentration. The enzymes present naturally in the fruits and vegetables cause the ripening and work only at a warmer temperature range. Since the produce has to be frozen immediately and enzymes cannot act after chilling, the time has to be just right to pluck it. Even though some of the nutrients do get lost in the freezing process, most of the nutrition gets locked in when iced. Research has shown some batches of frozen fruits have more polyphenols than far-travelling fresh produce. The best way to consume fresh fruits and vegetables is to grow them in your kitchen garden or buying from a locally sourced *mandi* or open vegetable market. And that too should be consumed the same day. But in the real world of a self-reliant mother, you can reach for those frozen peas and carrots to get the best you can for yourself and your baby.

4. *Special foods: Must-haves for the new mother*

Every state in India has a specific customized diet for the new mother. Many of these foods are loaded with dry fruits and ghee. They play a special role in providing nourishment to the demands of recovery and breastfeeding. The *methi laddoos*, a staple for every breastfeeding mother, and the panjeri stand high on the list of must-have foods for women post-delivery. You can make *panjeri* and methi laddoos in your third trimester if you are going to be by yourself once the baby arrives. Panjeri is a mix of dry fruits, coconut, dates and jaggery lightly roasted in ghee. I used to soak it in hot milk and eat around dawn. They can be refrigerated in bulk and a few can be stored in a container and kept next to your bed. As a midnight snack you could just reach out for a methi ka laddoo on your night stand and you will get a wholesome power packed snack. Methi seeds are superb for increasing milk production, the jaggery in the laddoo a rich source of iron and *gond* is an excellent source of dietary fibre helping you to feel full and improving bowel movement. Ghee and gond both supply short chain fatty acids to the body and help in beneficial redistribution of body fat and promote metabolism. Gond is great for those recovering from gestational diabetes as it reduces fasting glucose levels and promotes weight loss.

One recipe that caught my attention was my friend Manu's Marwari miracle drink. Her mother-in-law would make a *khus khus* (poppy seeds) milk for her daily and she would be knocked out into the most blissful of daytime naps on drinking it. For those of you who are struggling to sleep when the baby sleeps, here is how to get some help with some quality shut eye:

- Soak 2 teaspoons of khus khus and 6 almonds overnight.
- Next morning, grind them together into a fine paste.
- Take a pan, add a teaspoon of *desi ghee* and roast the paste.
- Add a pinch of black pepper powder and cardamom powder to this mix. You could season with a little saffron too.
- Mix 2-3 teaspoons of this paste in 300 ml of hot milk and add sugar as per your taste. Drink up and pass out!

A great time to have this drink is after your daily *maalish*. The baby sleeps for a good two–three hours after the massage and the mother usually gets super ravenous after her own massage and bath. Instead of wasting time fixing lunch, this could be your filling snack. Drink up and sleep with your baby.

These days there are concerns raised about the morphine content of poppy seeds and how the mother and child could get addicted to it. What the internet fails to inform us is that the source of the addictive opium is not the seed but instead the sap of the poppy plant. It is true that some content of morphine is found in every part of this plant, but the edible seed has a tiny amount. In addition, soaking, washing and grinding of the poppy seeds further reduces this minute morphine content. I know people who are fully functional non-addicted adults after having consumed this poppy seeds drink regularly.

The advantages offered by poppy seeds pretty much know no bounds:

- Rich source of iron, phosphorus and calcium. Essential for blood formation and bone restoration.
- Excellent source of zinc which is necessary for healing as well as thyroid health.
- Provides the body with much needed magnesium, copper and manganese which are important for chemical balance in the postpartum brain.
- Improves fertility by enhancing fallopian tube health as well as restores sex drive in women. I know, now is not the time for thinking about more action but it's all a part of the recovery process and reclaiming your health.

- Protects from constipation because of high fibre content.
- The high oleic acid and Omega-6 fatty acid help restore balance to your blood pressure and are important for heart health.
- The antioxidants present are beneficial to the eyes and skin.

5. *Getting off the vegan bandwagon: The vegetarian diet versus the non-vegetarian diet*

Proponents of vegetarianism might not appreciate this part of my chapter. If it is against your principles to eat an animal then by all means, please don't let me convince you otherwise. A *sattvik* diet, where no animal is harmed, works great for postpartum healing, but a non-vegetarian diet has its own place in nourishing the mother's body. And since Ayurveda respects the mind, body and soul of every living being, no part of the animal is wasted (yes you can eat meat as per Ayurveda. It is called a *Tamasaik* diet). Even animal feet are cooked and have such a special place in postpartum meals (goat trotters which are called *paaya*, are one of the best non-vegetarian foods for the new mother). In Chinese culture, pig trotters are given to the woman after her delivery. These are simple to cook dishes and can be made easily by the woman who has a limited support system. The meat is not as important but leaching of the minerals from the bones of the animal (chicken or goat) by the process of prolonged cooking is the chief source of nourishment.

The benefits of bone broth are:

a. Gelatin from the bone broth supports healing of the mother's digestive system. The enlarged uterus, the medications and the anaesthesia (in case of caesarean) all have weakened the gut and it promotes sealing of the damaged intestines.
b. Breastfeeding takes minerals out of your bones to support the baby. Bone broth contains chondroitin and glucosamine which support bone remodelling. The gelatin present also helps in healing of the joints and prevents their degeneration. A woman's pelvic bones have been stretched and strained to support the baby during pregnancy. All of your body's joints are excessively relaxed for accommodating the growing baby by the hormone relaxin. These stand to benefit from the chondroitin content of the broth as they recover to the pre-pregnant state.
c. Pregnancy takes a toll on integrity of the gum tissue. The minerals in the broth help improve oral health in mothers by restoring gum strength.
d. The naturally available collagen in the broth restores skin plumpness and heals pregnancy skin. The high protein content of the broth or soup is required by the healing body of the new mother. The amino acid Proline promotes skin restoration. The other amino acids calm the mind, restore hormonal and chemical imbalances

that occur after delivery and help provide the mother with a refreshing sleep.

e. The bone broth is a rich source of calcium, iron and zinc. You will need an extra supply of these vital minerals during postpartum recovery and breastfeeding.
f. For those of you fretting about your weight right after delivery, please don't. You took 9 months to gain that body, give yourself at least 9 months to lose it. The broth is a rich source of protein and minerals and can be consumed with whole wheat roti. There is your soup for weight management and protein for fullness, if that's the kind of diet that makes you happy. You can also make the broth in advance and freeze it in an ice tray. Just take out few cubes, re-heat and voila!

I am advocating these wondrous Indian foods, because that is what I have been exposed to all my life. But then again there are millions of people worldwide, eating what is around them, cooking foods unknown to the Indian palate and thriving by being true to their heritage.

A study was done in China on rural practices of caring for the new mother. On the food practices in the Chinese villages, the research paper quotes: 'Foods such as fruits, vegetables, soybean products and cold drinks which are considered "cold" should be avoided. In contrast foods such as brown sugar, fish, chicken and pig's trotter which are considered "hot" should be encouraged.'[1]

I began this chapter by stating how a woman suffered from poor health because of unjustified food restrictions by the aunt in the name of hot foods and cold foods. The message of my book is that no single authority is always right or always wrong. The researchers go on to justify that they undertook this study to educate new mothers about the importance of fruits and vegetables to prevent constipation and piles that was so prevalent among the rural women. The villagers also ignored oral hygiene after delivery and the researchers educated them with regards to that. Getting to know the roots of rural practices and discouraging the wrong ones are steps in the right direction for sure. In fact, the villagers adhered to the medical advice imparted to them and benefited from the researchers' interventions.

However, there are two sides to a coin. These researchers seemed to have missed out on a nugget of truth by calling all of the Chinese rural practices universally ignorant or superstitious. One particular food item which caught my eye in this research paper was soybean. It was not allowed to a woman who had just delivered because the food was considered to be cold. And if we could just open our eyes and look beyond the protein content of soybean, perhaps we can find some logic behind this food restriction.

6. *Legumes: Avoid them in the postpartum period*

The advice of not giving soybean to a new mother can be broken down into two parts:

- It's a cold food
- Don't give it to a woman who has just delivered

Back in the day when I was as arrogant as any science fanatic, I too winced whenever I heard my patients talk of cold foods and body heat. I saw that it was one of the most prevalent beliefs in the patient community and rather hard to shake off. Science completely rejects the idea of heating and cooling foods and devotes little attention to dietary modifications for changing seasons, growth spurts and the postpartum state. It takes full-fledged diabetes or a failing kidney for a doctor to pay attention to the patient's eating habits.

There are so many processes at play before a food reaches your plate and soy is no exception. Soybean is cultivated in summers and its flower blossoms in winter. The change of season that occurs in temperate regions such as China is vital for the flowers because they only bloom when the sun shines for less than twelve hours. By the time summer season is back, it is ready for consumption. In fact, a scientist by the name Andrew McClung tried to grow soybean in the Cerrado region (a place in Brazil). Brazil, being in the tropical belt, does not experience a marked difference in summers and winters. The plant failed to grow much in height and ended up being a stunted version of itself. Nonetheless, McClung was awarded the WHO food prize in 2006 for removing soybean from its natural habitat, planting it in a place where it did not belong and breeding a stunted hybrid variety that was no way close to the original.

Another study on the metabolism and absorption of soybean in horses showed that the excreted byproduct of soy, *equol*, was found abundantly in the urine of female horses (mares) in summers and negligible in winters. The bacteria needed to digest soy in the horse gut seemed to function only in summers.

But nonetheless, soybean is a great source of protein. Great for a new mom who is breastfeeding, right? Wrong! The Chinese grannies really had it all figured out when they stopped their new mothers from eating soybean. The unfavourable effects of soybean on a new mother are due to the following anti-nutritional factors:

a. The Phytates: These components present in soybean, interfere with the absorption of essential minerals such as iron and calcium. It is an anti-nutritional factor and will prevent your gut from absorbing minerals. For instance, a patient suffering from anemia (due to lack of iron) is always advised to have tea (which is abundant in another anti-nutritional factor called tannin) at least two hours after meals to allow for adequate iron absorption from the food. (We don't put a blanket ban on tea in anemics just because it has tannins.) Phytates per se aren't bad and in fact are a rich source of the mineral phosphorous (has an important role in cell functioning).
b. The Isoflavones: This component present in soybean has an oestrogenic effect on the female body. Oestrogen reduces milk production in the new mother. It is for this

reason that a breastfeeding mother is not given birth control pills because of its high oestrogen content. So, moms, please put down that tofu pizza.

c. Anti-thyroid Hormone Production: One of the natural effects of excess soybean consumption is inhibition of thyroid hormone production. Eating foods such as soybean right after delivery will mess with the rising thyroid hormone and declining oestrogen. Thyroid hormone promotes increase in metabolism and takes care of your skin, hair and bones after delivery. Restrict soybean in your meal for the first six weeks at least after delivery till your metabolism gets on the right track.

However, don't go up in arms to ban soy from all foods. It has an excellent protein profile. Any food should be taken in moderation and not on a daily basis. Eat some, share some and all will be good.

We have our own version of soybean ban in India for the new mother. It's the *chana daal*. It is popularly called Garbanzo beans or chickpea in the West. Legumes, even though a great source of plant protein, need to be avoided for a couple of weeks after delivery because of the isoflavones, phytates and anti-thyroid action. These also make the woman gaseous and uncomfortable and are a little hard to digest. The important thing to remember while eating legumes is that the anti-nutritional components such as phytates are destroyed by wet heat (cooking at high temperatures in water). So be sure to pressure cook your *chhole*! Nonetheless, it is better to resume eating legumes after at least 2-3 months post-delivery.

Meal Plans

Before breakfast:

In my house, there is a special pre-breakfast drink my mother-in-law used to prepare for me. It helps in recovery and boosting immunity of the mother. I totally hated these drinks, so out of solidarity, my husband gave me company drinking them. Only because *you got to do what you got to do* and drink what you have to if you want to stay healthy.

The first 3 days: Neem Juice

How to prepare it:
Soak neem leaves in hot water, blend and strain. Absolutely bitter and disgusting to drink. But great for postpartum healing!

The next 3 days: Gond (edible gum) drink

How to prepare it:
Soak 1 tbsp gond in one glass of water overnight. Boil this gond water mixture along with some jaggery till it reduces to three-fourth its quantity. Add half a teaspoon of ghee and serve hot. It's a little thick to drink, so take your time sipping it. Gond boosts milk production and improves postpartum metabolic function.

The next 3 days: Halim (garden cress seed) drink

How to prepare:

Soak 1 tsp of Halim seeds overnight in one glass of water. Boil this halim water mixture along with some jaggery till it reduces to three-fourth the quantity. Add half a teaspoon of ghee and serve hot. This was one of the easiest to gulp down. It is an excellent source of calcium, iron and folic acid, so drink up. You can continue with these drinks for as long as you like as they are quite filling and are a great source of much-needed minerals.

The main meals of the day:

Here I have outlined meal options for you for a week. Everyone has different dishes as per their culture and this list is just a sample. Eat what suits you, keep a lookout for foods that aggravate your baby and avoid those for the first six weeks. Cabbage and potatoes are notorious for making breastfed babies gassy in the first few weeks so are best avoided in the postpartum period.

Be sure to follow up your lunch and dinner with the post-meal digestive (the ajwain, saunf, methi, kalonji seed mix). In addition, make a dry flaxseed *chutney* as an accompaniment to your lunch and dinner. To make it, roast one cup flaxseed, four dry Kashmiri chillies and a few garlic cloves together in a pan. Let the roasted mix cool and add salt and grind in a dry grinder. Have one teaspoon daily with your lunch. A great source of Omega-3 fatty acids and excellent for your little baby's brain development.

Monday
Breakfast: Fried egg with ghee paranthas
Lunch: Rice/Roti with cooked spinach (*palak sabzi*)
Dinner: Chicken stew with roti/*Masoor daal* with ajwain parantha

Tuesday
Breakfast: *Ragi* porridge with ghee and jaggery
Lunch: Paaya broth with roti or rice/Mix vegetable *Dalia*/porridge with ghee
Dinner: Same as lunch (since paaya takes long to cook and can be made in bulk)/Drumstick curry with roti or rice

Wednesday:
Breakfast: Egg dosa
Lunch: *Moong* sprouts stir fried with roti
Dinner: Khichdi with fried fish/Spinach khichdi

Thursday
Breakfast: Idli with sugar (avoid spicy sambar in the first few weeks and enjoy your idli with ghee and sugar)
Lunch: Bottle gourd stir fried/curry with roti/rice
Dinner: Egg curry with rice/roti/Dill leaves (*soa*) cooked with roti

Friday
Breakfast: Onion poha
Lunch: Moong dal with cooked fenugreek (*methi sabzi*) with roti/rice

Dinner: Lamb mince with roti/Tomato *rasam*, cooked apple gourd (*tinda sabzi*) with rice/roti

Saturday
Breakfast: Palak/Methi parantha
Lunch: Fish curry with rice/Cooked bitter gourd (*karela sabzi*) with roti
Dinner: Stir fried mixed vegetables (peas, capsicum, carrots) with roti

Sunday
Breakfast: *Upma*
Lunch: Vegetable pulao with cucumber salad
Dinner: *Matar paneer* with rice/roti

Go-to breakfasts on difficult days:

1. Milk oats with dry fruits (almonds, dates, raisins).
2. Packaged cereal with milk. Add nuts and dates for improving nutrient profile.
3. Eggs and bread.
4. Protein bars/Health bars/Granola bars (I know most days will be difficult with a newborn so please keep these kinds of protein bar breakfasts to a minimum and eat a healthy homemade breakfast).

Midday/Midnight snack

If you are going to be looking after yourself after delivery, then make a stock of laddoos and panjeri in your last trimester and stock in your refrigerator.

1. Khus khus almond milk (recipe given under 'special foods')
2. Methi laddoo
3. Gond laddoo
4. Rawa laddoo
5. Few almonds and dates
6. Upma: Easy to cook and filling for days you are tired of snacking on sweet items
7. Panjeri soaked in warm milk
8. Apple and a glass of milk
9. Tahini halwa with roti/bread (this halwa is a prepackaged halwa found in grocery stores in the middle east. If someone is travelling there, then ask them to get you a box or two. Tahini is made from sesame and is excellent for milk production. It could be one of your goto snacks when you are pressed for time.)
10. Roasted fox nuts (*makhana*): For days you are sick of laddoos and want something crunchy, go for this snack. Light roast in ghee with a pinch of salt and your protein-rich snack is ready. It is an excellent booster of milk production and can be incorporated into *kheer* too.

3

LOOKING AFTER THE NEW BABY

Taking care of your bundle of joy is often about picking and choosing from common sense, traditional wisdom and science. Often, it is just a matter of going by your gut but it is best to stay informed.

At the Hospital

The first hour after birth

1. Pre-lacteal feeds:

   It is a common cultural practice to give something sweet to a newborn baby right after birth, before breastfeeding is initiated. This custom is known as a pre-lacteal feed (pre – before, lacteal – milk) and is a food rich in sucrose. In North India, a family member will apply honey on a gold ring and make the baby lick it. It is usually done by someone whose qualities the parents wish upon the newborn. A mantra is then read out into the baby's ear. This practice is called *ghuti pilana*. Another variant of this custom is to smear jaggery dipped in ghee on the baby's tongue in the shape of the symbol Om. Among Hindus in South India, sugar syrup is used instead. Among Muslims all over the world, the practice is to rub a softened date onto the baby's palate by a revered member of the family. This is known as *Tahneek*. Honey is used if dates aren't available.

This practice is losing popularity because of the doctor's disapproval of giving the baby anything besides the mother's milk in the first six months but the custom of giving a sugary pre-lacteal feed is very beneficial to the child. Delivery of the baby is as stressful an event for the baby as it is exhausting for the mother. A little bit of sucrose helps relieve the baby of the pain of passing through the birth canal and the stress of being examined by the paediatrician right after the birth. It brings down the respiratory rate and the heart rate. Giving the baby honey or sugar syrup before a needle prick or vaccination too will reduce the need of paracetamol that is often prescribed for these painful events.

The pre-lacteal feed has a special significance in the case of premature babies. Babies delivered prematurely are often admitted in ICUs for low blood sugar levels. These tiny little babies have IV sets poked and strapped onto their delicate hands to manage their feeds through an intravenous line. A cheap and effective way of managing low blood sugar levels in these preemies is by using a dextrose gel placed in their mouths (a softened date is the cheaper option to achieve the same result).

Science has objected to giving dates to the newborn because the date could be contaminated with dangerous bacteria, but according to custom the relative softens the date in his own mouth before giving it to the baby. Saliva is rich in Immunoglobulin A (an antibody). So, the person who is putting the date into the baby's mouth is also providing the baby with antibodies against any contamination. Even in the case of honey, if given the right way, one need not worry about contamination with botulism causing bacteria (a very dangerous bacterium found in dust). If the mother is going to initiate breastfeeding in the next hour or two, the baby will get antibodies from the mother's milk against any clostridial spores that have contaminated the honey.

On the other hand, many parents and grandparents don't stop at giving the sugar solution as the first feed. It is a common belief that the first milk the mother gets is impure and a waste and the mother isn't allowed to breastfeed for the first three to six days. This is where wisdom ends, and ignorance begins. Pre-lacteal feed is to be treated as just that – something that needs to be given just before beginning breastfeeding. The baby should be brought to the mother's breast after that.

2. Breastfeeding and skin to skin

The next phase in newborn care is breastfeeding. I have detailed its various aspects and challenges in Chapter 5. As a caesarean patient myself, breastfeeding was initiated for me in the first hour after delivery. Even though I was numb from the waist down (because of spinal anaesthesia) and I couldn't move a muscle, it did not stop my babies from getting what was rightfully theirs. The nurses would tug my breast all the way to the baby lying by my side and helped in initiating breastfeeding.

A new mother and child need physical contact more than observation in an incubator. The respiratory rate normalizes as well as his depth of respiration picks up just by skin-to-skin contact with the mother. For distressed babies and preemies, the best way to maintain body temperature and breathing is by placing the baby between the mother's breasts and allowing breastfeeding on demand. This practice is called Kangaroo mothercare because the baby is kept in a chest to chest position with the mother and they look like baby and mommy kangaroos. KMC has been shown to decrease mortality and morbidity in preterm and low birth-weight infants by providing protection from infection; regulating temperature, breathing, and brain activity; and encouraging mother–baby bonding.

And it is not just the baby who needs the mother. The mother needs the baby more than the baby needs her. You ask how? Before I answer that let me put forward a few facts:

1. The mother is given a dose of Pitocin (artificial oxytocin) after the delivery of the placenta for her uterus to contract and reduce bleeding after delivery.

2. An oxytocin surge is natural during the first hour after delivery.
3. Nipple stimulation is one of the biggest stimulators of oxytocin production.
4. Oxytocin is the main hormone responsible for bonding between a mother and child.

If the mother and child are left together, then the mother's bleeding after delivery will be reduced naturally if breastfeeding is initiated rather than by an artificial drip. Pitocin is given in a diluted form in the saline drip. The amount of intravenous fluids to be given to the mother will also be less if the dose of Pitocin is reduced and if the natural oxytocin produced in the mother's body by sucking is relied upon. Too much of IV fluids makes the breasts balloon out, the nipples flatten, and this makes it difficult for the baby to latch on. The first one hour is great for the baby and the mother to look at each other, take in each other's beautiful image and imprint on each other. Oxytocin has an amnesic as well as analgesic (pain killer) effect on the mother. It helps her forget the birth trauma sooner. The reward of her labour being in her arms makes the discomfort and pain of the episiotomy or caesarean wound easier to tolerate.

The most insensitive aspect of delivery in the West has been baby nurseries in the hospitals where all the babies are put together in a room in their individual cribs and they could wail away to their heart's content, stressing each other out. In a town in Germany, it was recognized for centuries that the baby being in contact with the mother after birth caused her uterus to contract. The uterine contractions were thought to be a nuisance rather than beneficial to the mother. It was their custom to not allow the mother and child to sleep next to one another in the first twenty-four hours after delivery. They would say, 'If the mother and child are together, the uterus can find no rest and scratches about in the woman's body, like a large mouse.'[1] Their observation was on point but conclusion totally wrong. These uterine contractions in fact help in reducing the enlarged uterus back to normal and reduce the amount of blood lost after delivery.

The First 24 to 48 Hours: Baby Pee and Poop

If you are already a parent or know a neurotic-baby-obsessed parent, you know I am not exaggerating the importance parents place on their baby's poop. The first newborn stool is happily welcomed, and the granny gleefully wipes off the sticky goo from the baby's skinny bottom (yes, all newborns have skinny butts). Grandmothers have left newborns diaper-less, waiting with bated breath for the first pee. Many parents have shrieked with joy on seeing their one-week old baby producing yellow poop for their first time in his life and their happiness is only one step behind an Oscar acceptance speech.

The baby's pee and poop are very good indicators of the baby's hydration, nourishment and overall health, the first ones being particularly important. A newborn should pass stools in the first twenty-four hours after birth and urine in the first forty-eight hours. The first few stools, called meconium, are dark green to black in colour and are sticky in consistency. The closest description available in medical books is the word 'tarry'. The junk that's been accumulating in your baby's intestine during the duration of pregnancy is passed in this first stool. The baby swallows its wispy hair and shed skin cells along with amniotic fluid inside the uterus. The first stool is proof that the baby's digestive tract is in continuity. Very rarely, babies don't have an anal opening and such a condition needs surgery. The passing of meconium is nothing short of great news.

The first pee though is a discreet business. Disposable diapers these days are so quick in absorbing and the newborn's urine volume so little that it is hard to merely look at the diaper and figure out if the baby has peed. Medical guidelines suggest waiting for forty-eight hours for the first urine. Make sure you watch out for both urine and stools to tell your paediatrician when she/he comes for your baby's checkup before discharge.

A Night in the Life of the Mother and Baby

The nursery

In today's world, a child doesn't have to become a teenager to claim his own room and privacy. The popular concept of the baby nursery with beautifully painted walls with rainbows and storks are not only commonplace in the West but have also found a market in India. With bigger paycheques, come bigger houses and bigger distances between new moms and newborns. There was once a time when the mother would make a *jholi* or a swing out of her saree and let the baby sleep in it during the day and in the safety of her arms during the night, but gone are those days.

So, what is the best place and best method to put the baby to sleep?

The self-proclaimed baby sleep expert Richard Ferber came out with a Bible for sleep training tiny babies in the 1980s. In his book he says that a child is emotionally ready for sleep training anywhere between three and five months of age.[2] The mother is supposed to feed and have a 'loving bed time routine' before leaving the baby in his crib. The baby is allowed to 'cry it out' till he falls asleep. If the baby cries too much, then the mother is advised to step into his room to pat him and comfort him by her voice alone but not pick him up, was what Ferber advised. The baby's crying episodes are gradually phased out to be longer and longer till he learns to self-soothe and fall asleep on his own. This practice of crying it out and self-soothing got so popular that it was a nationwide practice in the US and sleep training a baby came to be known as Ferberizing.

Co-sleeping is widely frowned upon in the West. Even though the value of breastfeeding is regaining its importance and more mothers are opting for it, there is much to be desired. Separate bedrooms are a recipe for early breastfeeding discontinuation (in the first three–four months most commonly). Feeding a separately sleeping baby requires too much effort as the mother has to get up, feed, put the baby back to sleep and tiptoe away. Many a times, the baby will wake up even before the mother has left the room and cry for her. Sleep deprivation is bad enough and listening to your baby howl night after night is even more traumatic. It is easier for the mother to take turns with the husband for the night shift (who is going to bottle feed) pushing breastfeeding into the background.

'Baby care scientists' advise against co-sleeping and urge the mothers to maintain a distance with their babies. As observed by child psychologists Mary Ainsworth and John Bowlby, babies who are held, carried and have their nurturer close by tend to be more well-rounded, easily adjusting and more trusting of their parents. These babies are said to be 'securely attached' to their caregiver. But shockingly, mothers are encouraged to *not* follow their instincts and harden up towards their children. Eventually weaker bonds are formed between the baby and mother allowing the mothers to leave their kids in their separate rooms without remorse. This leads to children who have no feelings of security right from a tender age. In their impressionable minds no importance has been placed on motherly affection and family bonds. They grow up to be 'insecurely attached'. These 'good' sleep-trained babies are left to look after themselves and be disciplined from the age of just a few months. They are said to have weaker bonds with their mothers and are more prone to depression.

The mould of forming meaningful relationships was tampered with and the blank slate of the child's brain that could form bonds was scribbled upon illegibly by science. Studies show that such children grew up to be aggressive preteens, rebellious and detached teens, commitment-phobic young adults and contributed eventually to the rising divorce epidemic that took off in the late 20th century. Depression rates have gone through the roof as all the Ferberized infants are now adults. Parents are now confused as to why their kids won't trust them and talk to them. Eating disorders and self-worthlessness have rocketed because the children don't know who to turn to with their problems and have succumbed to peer pressure. They learnt rather young that mommy wasn't someone to seek for security and comfort. Eventually they were incapable of trusting and being trusted. A baby understands the language of touch more than the spoken word. So, assure him he is safe by holding him. If you don't hold your baby fearing you will 'spoil' him today, then be sure he is ruined for tomorrow.

Not only was the practice of co-sleeping of mother and child in the poor underdeveloped countries contributing to raising securely attached individuals, but there was also another effect of this practice – fewer number of Sudden Infant Death Syndrome (SIDS) deaths. SIDS or cot death is the sudden unexplained death of a baby in the cot. With Ferberization came the practice of exhausting and defeating the baby into the submission of sleep on his tummy. The prone sleep position put abnormal pressure on the brainstem (the part of the brain just above the neck region). The brainstem is responsible for regulating breathing. With the tummy position for sleep, the number of SIDS was at an all-time high. A lot of research into sleeping positions brought about the new campaign of 'Back to Sleep' in the early 1990s which is preached to this day. Parents were advised to put their babies to sleep on their backs as it was believed to protect against SIDS. And as a matter of fact, there has been a drop in the number of SIDS deaths in the US after that.

India is far from achieving an infant mortality rate to boast about but the number of SIDS deaths in India is very low compared to the US. Co-sleeping addresses all the problems that the debate around the ideal sleep position, and the mystery around SIDS, raises.

1. Sleeping with the mother regularizes the deep sleep and shallow sleep pattern of the baby. Even if the baby drifts off to a deep sleep it will be roused multiple times during the night by the mother's breathing and movements.
2. A 'sleep trained' baby falls into a deep fatigued sleep due to excessive crying. The deep sleep and inability to break free of the spells of shallow breathing or apnea (episodes of no breathing for short periods) makes a child prone to the risk of SIDS.
3. Pacifier seems to prevent SIDS by mechanism yet to be figured out, but if the baby is co-sleeping he will rise

two to three times in the night and feed and fall asleep on the breast. He has the protection offered by the best pacifier ever, his mother's breast.

4. The 'Back to Sleep' campaign asked parents to put their babies to sleep on their backs. Sleeping on the back brought down the mysterious SIDS death rate by half in the US in the 1990s but on the downside, this led to a whole generation which has grown up with the backs of their heads flattened. Sleeping with the mother eliminates this back sleeping or tummy sleeping problem. The mother and baby change positions multiple times in the night. For some part of the night he will be lying on his back. Sometimes he will fall asleep on the mother's chest after nursing. This allows for better body heat regulation, better respiration control, easily rousing with the mother (which protects against the dreaded deep sleep of SIDS). The change of positions doesn't allow abnormal pressure points on just one side of the head through the night and protects the head from developing flat spots.
5. Some people argue there is a risk of smothering when sleeping with the mother. This risk ranges from negligible to none in mothers who are mentally sane and are not under the influence of any intoxicating substances. In fact, the reported deaths due to smothering by a parent were due to mothers from extremely poor households deliberately killing their unwanted children by smothering them. They don't need to be made into a statistic. They need better birth control and social support.

Another risk of SIDS is sleeping with a smoker parent. The cigarette fumes continue to be exhaled by the parent after a smoke. A baby under the age of three months is particularly at risk of SIDS if sleeping next to a smoker parent. This statistic discouraged parents from co-sleeping when it should have discouraged them from smoking!

The mother–baby bond is a life-long relationship. If the foundation is solid, the mother and the child will enjoy a meaningful, symbiotic trusting relationship from birth till adulthood. The child goes on to feel secure no matter what life throws at him. We are asked to be deviant from nature in the name of scientific progress but science is robbing us of our intuition, our maternal instincts and from loving our children altogether.

When Days and Nights are All Mixed Up

Newborn babies have a tough time figuring out whether it is night or day. In the first two months, your baby will sleep at the oddest of hours and probably want to party in the night. It is very irritating for the mother at best and pure torture mostly but their internal body clock figures it out soon enough and by the third month things will start to look better in the sleep department. Some of the things which are believed to assist the baby in getting to know what the party timings during the day are:

1. **Morning sun exposure**: Most babies have mild physiological jaundice and sun exposure helps get rid of that. The gentle morning rays are a great source of Vitamin D without requiring the additional source from Vitamin syrups and drops. This also acquaints the body clock sooner with the concept that mornings are for staying up and night for restful sleep. The grandparents or parents or nanny can take turns taking the baby out in the sunshine early in the morning when the sun's rays are not harsh. Make sure the baby is well exposed to the sun and well protected from any wind. It's the sun's rays that affect the baby positively and not the sun's warmth.
2. **Dim lights in the night**: Many moms sleep with the lights on at night because they want to keep checking on the baby. If you are one of those moms, then please use a side table lamp or a dim light instead. After a month, hopefully you will be a pro at the game and will be more comfortable at night handling your baby. A side table lamp is a good investment for this source of light which will also help with midnight snacking and midnight diaper changes. I have slept with a dim light on after both my deliveries.
3. **Quieter at night**: As mentioned earlier, put the baby for a nap in the living room in a bassinet or a jholi rather than the secluded bedroom. If you have a crib, then wheel the crib outside the bedroom during daytime. Morning should be associated with the hustle and bustle

of day-to-day activities. Many new mothers, including I, let their firstborns sleep in pin drop silence only to regret it later. Such babies are extremely light sleepers and startle at any and every sound. Let their night sleep be quieter but day time naps should be accompanied by the sounds of the cooker whistling, birds chirping and you talking to the maid and *dhobi*.

A Day in the Life of the Mother and Baby

Grooming the baby

The baby is usually not bathed till discharge. If the baby is admitted in the hospital for a few days, then the nurse will bathe him in a tiny tub as per the doctor's orders. Baths are not necessary at first as a baby doesn't really get dirty and the protective cheesy covering on the body called vernix helps him in body temperature regulation. You could wait 3-4 days before starting a bathing routine.

In India, one of the most important preparations done before the baby's birth is hiring a masseuse. Popularly known as the *maalishwali*, the masseuse is a tough woman with hands of steel who does not flinch from deeply massaging a newborn into a long peaceful slumber daily. In earlier times, the maalishwali used to be a relative but these days she is usually a hired professional.

Massages are really important for newborn babies and here's why:

1. Preterm babies who are massaged regularly gain weight faster than the babies who are not given massages.
2. Babies massaged with a vegetable oil have fewer infections which occur in babies due to prolonged hospital stays. Preterm babies have an undeveloped skin barrier benefit more from the protection afforded by the oil.
3. There is absorption of oil through the baby's skin and that is a source of nourishment for the baby. Massaged babies gain weight partially due to increased blood triglyceride levels because of the oil application.

Some women question the need for a vigorous massage for a newborn. Babies seem to be distressed by it, some may argue. If the masseuse is an expert and doing it right, then the deep pressure applied is actually good for the babies but if you want to take a call whether the massage is any good then look out for the following:

1. If an elder in the house who has raised babies says the masseuse is good, then you can safely take their word for it.
2. How is the baby after the massage? Is he falling into deep sleep during the bath itself? Is the baby sleeping for long after the massage? If yes, then your masseuse is on the right track.
3. If you want to assess for yourself whether the massage is done right, watch out for these techniques:

Effleurage: Stroking the baby's muscle gently along the length. This is when the masseuse applies the oil on the baby's body.

Petrissage: It is pressure applied across the width of the muscle. You will see the masseuse holding the baby's limb with one hand and massaging around the circumference with the other hand.

Friction: Deep massage applied by circular motions of the thumbs or fingertips. This is when the masseuse will start applying deeper pressure to the baby. The baby will grunt in response to each stroke and maybe even cry out loud. Not something you should worry about.

Kneading: Squeezing across the width of the muscle. This is basically petrissage with deeper pressure. The masseuse will be squeezing and moving her hand across the baby's limb.

Tapotement: Light slaps or karate chops. The masseuse will end the massage with gently slapping across the baby's body and do light-pressured karate chops.

In the West, a hospital nurse or doula will show the parents how to massage the baby. They use very mild pressure and apply oil gently over the baby's body. I am happy that they are realizing the importance of touch for a baby's growth but sadly, their massage stops at gentle stroking techniques and doesn't involve deep pressure methods.

Or does it?

They are indeed doing the vigorous-massage-which-will-make-the-baby-cry in the West but a few months too late. Here's how:

A baby tends to develop flat spots on his head when made to sleep alone. This condition is called *Plagiocephaly*. A newborn baby can't roll over to his side on his own till the age of four to six months. That's a lot of time spent sleeping on the back. In addition, babies who are left alone in the nursery are also prone to turning their heads to one side while sleeping. This has not only led to the development of flat spots on one side of the head but also tightening of neck muscles on the opposite side, a condition called torticollis. The muscle affected in torticollis is the Sternocleidomastoid muscle (SCM for short). To feel this muscle, turn your head to one side and touch the long tight neck muscle that stands out on the opposite side.

Parents are confused as to why their babies favour this abnormal turning of head in their sleep. It is because of a strong rooting reflex in babies. If you have ever held a small baby, you would have noticed how the baby turned towards your breast in search of milk. Rooting is a reflex that is seen in normal newborn babies, where he automatically turns his face towards a stimulus when the cheek or lip is touched and tries to suck. This reflex ensures a baby's survival. Had it not been for it, breastfeeding would have been very difficult. A baby that is sleeping alone is reflexively turning towards one side in search of his mother.

Torticollis and plagiocephaly go hand in hand and parents have to seek treatment for both. Another bad news is that babies who develop flat spots on their heads show delayed development. Plagiocephalic babies are sent to practitioners who specialize in making customized baby helmets to apply constant pressure on the head and correct the abnormal flat spots. The baby is usually three to four months old when the problem surfaces. Babies with torticollis are given physical therapy where the therapist applies opposing pressure to the tight muscle to loosen it up. The procedure is painful for the baby, but it is important to do it at a young age when the tightness in the neck muscle is still reversible. Parents need to be tough through this difficult phase.

Co-sleeping solves the issue of the baby turning his head to only one side in his sleep. The mother has to often adjust her baby during the night and put him to sleep in different positions after nursing. The vigorous massage your maalishwali does for your delicate yet tough baby is the physical therapy the Westerners do for the neck muscles after the baby has already developed neck stiffness.

The Indian *Jholi*

I was gifted a jholi and it came with its stand and custom-made cloth sheets that could be easily fastened to the hooks on the stand. My daughter slept with me during the night and in the jholi during the day. The traditional

Indian jholi is a DIY swing of sorts for the baby to sleep in. A sheet of cloth is fastened to a support at the two ends and a pouch like bed is made for the baby. This may seem like the poor man's crib, but it does come with its inherent benefits.

1. When the baby is put in the jholi the cloth plunges down as it isn't a rigid surface. This shapeshifting bed is great for the development of a round head.
2. The baby feels cocooned in the jholi and sleeps much better during daytime naps. It functions similar to a swaddle but with less pressure on the chest.
3. The rocking motion of the jholi is great for the brain development of the infant. The part of the brain (the vestibular system in the inner ear) responsible for posture and maintenance of the body's balance is stimulated by the rocking motion.
4. Sleeping in a jholi makes the baby favour a flexed posture and prevents an extended back and neck that happens by sleeping flat on a bed. This flexed posture promotes normal motor development in a baby.

All shapeshifting beds aren't good for the baby though. Water beds have often resulted in deaths by entrapment or suffocation. The 'Back to Sleep' campaign of the 1990s is now replaced by the 'Safe to Sleep' campaign of the 2000s. In this campaign parents are advised to avoid excess bedding and water beds, to put the baby to sleep on his back and to use a pacifier. How about we remove all of those unnecessary campaigns and just start 'Next to Mom', 'Jholi for Nap' and 'Breastfeed at Night' campaigns. How many more babies need to die in their cots before those sleep scientists realize it is called 'cot' death for a reason?

The Indian Art of Making the Head Round

Aside from co-sleeping and the jholi, there is another intervention which makes the head round. A cotton cloth is tied around the circumference of the baby's head during the day which applies mild pressure from all sides on the soft mouldable baby head. Therapists are using baby helmets along the same principle in babies with plagiocephaly but with a more rigid material (as the baby is older and the head is less mouldable).

In fact, mothers of newborns are advised to gently press the head of the baby into a spherical shape while breastfeeding. A newborn's feeding sessions last over a good half hour. Spend five-ten minutes of that time gently massaging the baby's head into a round shape and that will prevent any flatness.

Bath Time

In India, maalishwalis have been bathing babies on their legs before the invention of plastic tubs and bath chairs. There are no assistants to help out either. The baby is made to lie on one's legs, given a deep massage and bathed in hot water. And it is the best way to do it. Even if the baby wriggles and resists, you can manoeuver your legs to get better control. In addition, you know exactly what your baby is feeling. If you missed checking the water temperature, the water pouring on your baby will come on your legs and you can adjust the temperature to your requirement. The baby is comfortable, and both your hands are free to oil and soap the baby and you won't miss any spots. Often to your pleasure, at the end of the bath the baby falls asleep by the time he is in the towel.

The procedure

Usually my sequence during massage and bath is: massage the baby's front, pull baby to sit for head and face massage and end with massaging the baby's back. Then lather the baby's back and head and wash it off, pull the baby to sit to wash his face and then end with washing his front. This sequence is very helpful because you don't have to manoeuver the baby again and again. Before you take the baby for a bath make sure that you have kept all clothes, diaper, powder, lotion, nappy cream ready.

- Boil neem leaves in water and add this to a bucket of warm water. The neem leaves protect the baby's skin from infections.
- Position the stool in such a place that your legs can stretch out in front of you and you have access to the

bucket too. Keep the soap, oil and bucket to your right (whichever is your dominant hand). The towel should be within reach so that you can quickly wrap the baby and not let him startle awake after a sedating bath session.

- Sit on the stool with your legs stretched in front with about half a foot distance between the legs. Start with placing the baby on his back. Massage the baby's chest and legs. At first apply oil gently and then increase the pressure. Avoid deep pressure on the tummy. Deep pressure can be applied to arms and legs. Massage the oil around the circumference of the arms and legs. Pull the arms across one another and gently apply a tugging pressure.
- Gently pull the baby to sit to massage his face and head. Pour oil generously on his fontanelle (the soft spot on top of the baby's head) and lightly massage it in. You will find that oil gets absorbed into the fontanelle if you apply slowly. Do not apply pressure on the fontanelle. After pouring oil on the fontanelle, spread the oil and massage the entire head.
- Next place the baby on his tummy on your legs to massage his back, legs and arms. Use deep pressure for the back massage. Once you are done with massaging the limbs, massage the soles of his feet gently.
- Lather the baby's back and wash off.
- The baby's head is gently tucked in between your legs, with his face down and his head is lathered. Water is poured using a mug and the soap washed off. While

pouring water over the head make sure you gently press on either ear pinna with your middle finger and thumb to prevent water from entering the baby's ears. The other hand can be used to pour water while you protect the ears. This position also ensures that the bath water runs over the baby's head yet does not enter the baby's nose.

- After you are done washing baby's back, make your baby sit on your lap. Stabilize the baby by holding the baby's neck and upper back. Apply soap on his face and wash it off with wet hands. Small babies get startled if water is poured on their head. So, scoop some water with your hand and remove the soap off their face. In the end use your finger and rub their gums to maintain oral hygiene.
- Next, turn the baby to lie on his back. Lather chest, arms and legs.

A baby's neck is short and barely visible. Moisture, sweat and dead skin accumulate in the folds of the neck. If not cleaned and powdered daily, baby can develop redness and infection. If you are still learning to bathe the baby, then clean the neck after their bath with a damp washcloth. The neck can be accessed by holding the baby's upper back and gently letting the head tip. They have partial head control so the head dips backwards exposing the neck area. Don't apply direct pressure on the neck. Lift the skin between your thumb and index finger and clean. Apply powder after you have dried the area.

The toe spaces also collect moisture and are prone to infections if not separated and cleaned. A chubby baby would collect sticky debris between the fat rolls of his arms and thighs too. My daughter collected that grime in the fold behind her knee too. Separate all these folds gently and clean.

– Wrap the baby in the towel immediately after the bath. Stabilize yourself and take your time getting up. If you have bad knees or back, ask someone to take the baby while you get up in your own sweet time.

When the baby is very little, he will often fall asleep during the bath itself. Wrap the baby in a warm blanket and let him continue sleeping. They have the soundest sleep post massage, so you can catch up on your sleep or household chores while he naps.

Bath chairs

I was gifted a bath chair for my first born by a relative. I am still not convinced about its utility. The problem with baby gear is that manufacturers keep producing new versions and the classic user-friendly design gets lost in the reboot. I was gifted the bath chair from the same company my relative had bought hers, but a newer version. The makers thought they were doing a great job at redesigning it, but I would beg to disagree. My three-month-old son was ready to jump out of it. It was very unstable and defeated the purpose of owning a bath chair because I needed my husband's help to stabilize the chair as well as the baby.

Pros of a bath chair

- Hands free to lather up the baby.
- Can be easily washed since it is made of flexible mesh material.
- Some people have opted for a tub for the baby. They fill it up and let the baby bathe in it. It is a slightly disgusting alternative for bath time because the baby pees in the tub and splashes that pee water while playing. So, bath chairs are a great alternative as the surface has holes to let the bath water drain.
- A big solace for moms with knee and back issues who cannot bend forward to bathe their babies on their legs.

Cons of a bath chair

- It is difficult to find the perfect design. They are not exactly cheap so you cannot keep buying newer ones till you find the perfect fit.
- Cannot be used for newborns. The baby needs to achieve partial neck control at least.
- Some of them have a mechanism which is difficult to open by an adult but extremely easy to fold close by a baby sitting in it!

- Babies cannot be left unattended for even a second while bathing.
- Bathing the baby on your legs offers very good control over the baby. Even when the baby gets bigger and tries to crawl off, you can adjust your legs a little to get a grip on the squirmy baby. You have four limbs to control your kid rather than two. And for those wriggly babies, you need all the limbs you can get!

Baby Oil

A baby's skin is very sensitive and undeveloped. To decide what to apply on your baby's skin till the age of three months, use this rule of thumb: *Would you eat or drink this oil? No? Then don't expose your baby's skin to it.*

It's really a very simple mantra I am giving you. The baby's skin barrier is extremely delicate. One of the principles of Unani medicine and now emerging field of use of botanicals in skin care is that 'if it is safe to eat, then it is safe to apply.'

So how do you go about selecting the baby oil?

- Opt for a locally-produced oil. If you have been crazily using olive oil because the white man does it, then stop. It is not bad for the baby but there are big doubts regarding the purity of the available brands in the market nowadays.
- Coconut, sunflower, sesame or mustard oil are wonderful for baby massage.
- Don't use perfumed baby oils.

Do watch out for reactions in the baby. The baby's skin absorbs the oil. It has been proved that after massage, the baby's blood shows higher level of fatty acids from the oil and these help in his/her weight gain. You are basically feeding your baby through his skin. So, respect his tastes too.

The scoop on olive oil

Olive oil is wonderful no doubt but stop buying it unless you want to put it in Mediterranean cooking. Due to the outrageous global demand for olive oil in the last few decades, many no-gooders have entered the market, printed labels of 'Extra Virgin' and 'Cold pressed' and are selling you garbage in the name of Italian produce olive oil. If you wish to know more about this whole scam on olive oil, I would recommend that you read *Extra Virginity* by Tom Mueller.

Baby Soap

When I had started writing my book, I had one favourite brand of baby soap that I had used for both my babies. I wanted to give ancient wisdom a fair chance through every aspect of baby care, so I decided to dig deep into the traditional ubtan used for babies. My mother-in-law would give the maalishwali an ubtan paste to bathe my daughter with. It was made of half tablespoon besan atta (gram flour), half tablespoon jowar atta (sorghum flour) and a pinch of turmeric made into a thick paste with water. The first two days I kept my mouth shut and watched the procedure while my brain screamed the words 'SKIN IS SENSITIVE!' and 'ALLERGIES!' but when I heard the two ladies discuss that this regimen would make my baby fairer and have less hair, I put my foot down and didn't allow any of those ladies to body shame my beautiful daughter!

As always, I stand humbled.

Of course, I discovered my mother-in-law was right. Gram flour as a skincare product has positive research support for its antioxidant, anti-proliferative, and cancer protective activities. It has been used to reduce hyperpigmentation, enhance skin elasticity, control oil production, moisturize the skin, and delay hair regrowth (sorry, Maria, for the future waxing sessions you will have to endure. Your mother didn't listen to Dadi).

The baby's skin is still immature and developing rapidly. Any chemical offenders in the form of perfumes in baby products have the potential to mutate these cells. And whatever you apply on the skin gets absorbed through it and enters the bloodstream.

Reserve the use of soap in case of skin conditions (such as Dermatitis) on the recommendation of your doctor. If the baby's skin is healthy, then use homemade ubtan for the first three months or till the baby starts to crawl and collect germs from around the house.

Baby Lotion

Even though I did end up using a perfumed baby soap, one thing I am proud of is that I have never used any moisturizer on my baby's skin. Not because I am an organic momma but because my son likes to lick skin creams and lotions and my husband ends up hiding the bottle in the loft where he cannot reach. The lotion bottle was out of reach for all persons below the height of 5'10". I was left with no choice really.

I used an ayurvedic oil when she got a little bigger and she seemed to tolerate it well. It had an unusual smell but after washing with soap the smell was toned down. My baby never really smelled like a baby after her bath. She smelled like that ayurvedic oil. In fact, I never really removed the oil entirely by excessive lathering with soap. I moisturized her during her bath with oil and let it stay. To this day she has had no dry skin or skin irritation aside from the occasional diaper rash and one episode of cradle cap. Her skin is always soft and supple.

Diapering the baby

The girl diaper

A baby girl is affected by the maternal hormones more obviously than a boy. You will be shocked to find some vaginal bleeding in your little baby's diaper. It is completely normal and expected. Some babies have a pinkish discharge while some have a few drops of frank red blood in their diapers daily for a few days after birth. This can go on for the first two to three weeks to settle on its own. The baby was used to having your high oestrogen levels in her bloodstream when she was in the womb. After delivery, the hormone withdrawal causes this period-like-phenomenon in the baby (your periods also occur due to the hormone withdrawal which happens each month when pregnancy doesn't occur). You can expect adult-like white discharge too. To clean the white discharge, gently retract the labia (folds) with your fingers and wash away the collected discharge during the baby's bath time.

One important point to bear in mind is that cleaning a girl baby's bottom is very different from cleaning a boy baby's. For a girl, always ensure that you wipe or wash from front to back. That is from the urinary opening towards the anal opening. If you do it the other way, then you risk introducing faecal bacteria into the urinary opening and causing a urine infection.

Week 2 – Taking a call after the poop turns yellow

Cloth diapers OR Disposable diapers

In this increasingly eco-conscious world, more people are turning their backs on the extremely absorbent and conveniently disposable diapers to save the planet. While disposable diapers boast of less mess and drier nights, the washable ones are catching up too. Gone are the days when a *langot* (a diaper shaped cloth) was used as a diaper, with old cotton cloth as the absorber. These days there are Velcro fastening reusable diapers with absorbable inserts. The convenience factor is also not far behind. Rather than handwashing diapers after each time the baby wets it or soils it, a dedicated bin is kept for collecting diaper inserts over a couple of days and washing it all in one go in the washing machine. In the West, there are reusable-diaper-washing services which collects your dirty diaper load and supplies you with clean ones.

The disposable diaper camp

It is easy and convenient. You don't have to get invested in your child's poopy business more than you already are. Less effort and time go into doing laundry (you are probably doing a ton of laundry already). Travel and night-time are as easy as it could get. It is basically throwing money at the problem with little effort from your end. And in case the baby is having loosies, disposable diapers are a blessing.

The cloth diaper camp

1. **Cost:** You will have to buy 20-30 diapers in one go and they are way pricier than a single disposable diaper (the cost of a single disposable diaper is anywhere from ₹11–19 per piece whereas the cloth diapers is about ₹400–600 per piece) but that is a single time investment. There is only one standard size for cloth diapers and you can use the same twenty–thirty cloth diapers over the next two years or till whenever your baby is potty trained.

The total cost of disposable diapers till your baby is ready to go diaper free can come up to a staggering ₹40,000. If you invest in reusable diapers then the cost comes up to less than ₹14,000.

2. **The environment-friendly option:** There is no doubt that disposable diapers are one of the biggest occupants of the waste landfills in the world. A baby uses close to 3,000 diapers till it is toilet trained (yes, I did the math). On the other hand, the baby uses the same twenty to thirty cloth diapers in those first years till he is toilet trained. So, it may seem like we are saving the planet one diaper at a time but researchers delving deep into the making of cloth diapers have voiced their concerns over how thirsty the cotton crop is. Some also claim that the carbon footprint from the production and waste of all the disposable diapers is less than the carbon footprint of the electricity and water that go into the production and washing of the reusable diapers.

   Another thing to keep in mind is that the chemicals used in disposable diapers are said to be carcinogenic and linked to toxic shock syndrome. Diaper producers argue that the quantity is very small. More studies are needed to evaluate the risk.

3. **Earlier potty training:** These days disposable diapers are so highly absorbent that even when the diaper is super loaded with pee, the baby is comfortable. The baby does not feel the need to communicate his diaper needs to his mom. Cloth diaper babies are more willing to be

potty trained because of the discomfort that comes with wetness of the diaper. Also, the mothers of cloth diaper babies are more motivated to achieve potty training to lighten the laundry load. A disposable diaper mom, on meeting a hurdle, is more likely to give up potty training her kid to retry a few months later.

On one occasion my daughter did a poop mid-meal in her diaper. We were both watching TV and she didn't even seem uncomfortable. On getting a whiff of her nasties, I washed her and left her in underwear to continue with the meal. After sitting on my lap for some time she looked at me angrily and grunted. Not understanding what she was scolding me for, I let her go. She seemed to just want to walk off. I trailed after her with a morsel in my hand and almost slipped on her pee. It was then that I figured out she was asking me to let go of her because she needed to pee. The same child who was comfortable in her poop just ten minutes ago!

In this scenario, I was the bad mother who turned on the television and her one-year-old baby ate her meal while sitting in her own excrement. But when the same child, after a clean-up, was brought back to the same television without the super-absorbable diaper, she scolded her mother to let her get off the lap to go pee. The only factor that had changed was the diaper. The skin is the largest organ in the human body and it needs to be stimulated by the comfort of the mother's breast and the discomfort of a wet nappy for the little one to develop and speak.

The number of children affected by speech delay has steadily risen in the recent past. One in every 200 kids is affected by some form of language development delay in India. The easiest culprit to blame is the rising use of TV and gadgets. Kids who are singing nursery rhymes like it's no big deal are often clocking in more TV hours than their counterparts who aren't talking at the age of three. So, one can't put the blame on screen time only. There are many other factors. The family structure which is way different from just the previous generation has to take some of the fall. When the child was raised by grandparents, uncles, aunts and among cousins, he was more likely to pick up on conversations all day long. It does take a village to raise a child. The modern-day mother works outside and at home, buys her own groceries, does her own laundry and needs to find a vent while WhatsApping to her other mommy friends. I am one of them. I need a break from my kid's mischief because there isn't a village to entertain my child while I cook my meals. In a nuclear family, the television sometimes works as the village and is it so bad if the sole caretaker of the child wants to catch a breath every once in a while?

It is up to you to decide what options work best for you. If you are a working mother or have your hands full with older children, then you can go for the disposable option.

Or maybe you can mix it up a bit. You can use both to reduce the cost and ecological burden. Maybe cloth diapers during the day and disposable at night or when you go out. Perhaps your kid is already a year old and you don't feel like investing in cloth diapers when you have almost crossed the half way mark to toilet training. It's okay to continue with the disposable option in that case. Keep the eco-friendly option handy, however, when dishing out free advice to other expectant moms.

Cloth diapering

1. For the first two weeks when you are handling things, use newborn size disposable diapers. The meconium in your first week will cause nasty stains on the cloth diapers which don't wash away. Give yourself time to settle a bit before you take up the challenge of the laundry load.
2. If you have decided to go for cloth diapers, then buy your stock in your pregnancy days. It will be hard to find the motivation to buy and use cloth diapers when you are struggling to keep your life together after a new baby.
3. Kinds of cloth diapers:
    a. Cover diaper: The cover diaper looks like a padded nappy and you need to put a cotton liner in the crotch area. The cloth insert will come directly in contact with baby's skin. Not favoured by most moms as it moves about and gets wet and uncomfortable sooner.

There is another mix and match option available. You can use disposable nappy liners with a cover diaper. I would recommend using this option during the day or during the baby's poop time. All you need to wash is the wet diapers and not the poop ones. The poop filled liner can be just disposed off but if your kid poops at a different time each day, then it is not so advantageous for you.

b. The insert pocket diaper: The other option is the one with insert pocket. This diaper requires the insert material to be tucked inside. The insert and diaper are washed after separating. The insert is made of materials such as microfiber, muslin, bamboo, hemp or cotton.
c. The all-in-one diaper: Some diapers come with inserts and are washed together in bulk. These can also be used with disposable liners in the crotch area to increase absorbing capacity especially during the night.

4. One system you can adopt is washing the diaper load every third day. Buy a dustbin with a good secure lid and keep it in a secluded spot such as the laundry room or an unused balcony to keep the stink away. After each nappy change, throw the diaper in the bin. You can have a small dustbin in your room to dispose nappies changed during the day and throw collected diapers in the big bin at the end of the day. If you are using inserts, then make

sure you separate the insert and the nappy. If your baby has pooped, then wash away the gunk under running water before disposing off the diaper in the collecting bin. Whenever you think you need to wash the load, use a good quality detergent and some antiseptic and wash your diapers. Keep them out to dry preferably in the sun for better antibacterial protection.

Do keep a tiny stock of disposable diapers in case you cannot do your diaper laundry on time or the laundry doesn't dry up soon enough.

Cloth diapers do seem superior in terms of lesser burden on the pocket and less waste accumulation in our landfills but the people debating online what is best for the environment are not going to come and hold your fussy baby while you do the laundry. In the nuclear family setup, where a new mother is struggling to feed herself a nutritious meal and get some sleep, maybe just being able to throw away her baby's poop diapers along with her worries is the best option for her.

Swaddles

Swaddling was an undisputed way of clothing babies till about the 18th century. It was only recently that people have questioned its utility. The more people got educated, the more they replace wisdom with such counter-intuitive information.

Why swaddle?

1. Swaddling mimics the snugness of the womb: The baby was used to having pressure envelope him in the womb and those were the best days of the baby's life. There was no cold air jolting him awake, no need to poop and no need to cry for food. A swaddle eases the baby into living independently so to speak.
2. Swaddled babies sleep better: Swaddling makes the baby feel secure and reduces the startle reaction.
3. Swaddled babies are safer: In my subsection on co-sleeping, I mentioned that the 'Back to Sleep' campaign reduced the risk of sudden infant deaths by half. Swaddling a baby ensures that the baby can sleep on his back for longer.

The mechanism by which swaddling protects against SIDS is by reducing cortical arousals and facilitating subcortical arousals. If you have ever seen a newborn sleep, you will know how frightening their breathing and blinking pattern is. Sometimes the baby goes still and stops breathing to be followed by shallow rapid breaths. The eyes flutter rapidly to be followed by total stillness which is followed by a startled expression. I have been scared on seeing my daughter go through these phases and would feel for her heartbeat at the end of these episodes like a paranoid neurotic mother. But we moms are paranoid and neurotic about the well-being of our children so here is the low-down on what's happening during the baby's sleep.

A baby starts off with light sleep and drifts into deeper sleep states. Technically, these are divided into stage 1, 2, 3 of Non-Rapid Eye Movement (NREM) sleep and Rapid Eye Movement (REM) sleep but because you and I are not sleep scientists, let's call it quiet sleep and REM sleep. The same sleep cycle is also present in adults. Adults too, get up multiple times during the night to change their position, cover themselves or remove the covers. These tiny awakenings don't usually disturb our sleep. We smoothly progress from quiet sleep to dreamy (REM) sleep, wake up, roll over and go right back to sleep without getting aware of our wakefulness. Even our breathing pattern changes through the night from shallow breaths to deep breaths but it is not as pronounced as in babies.

In case of swaddled babies, the snugness and pressure of the swaddle prevents arousals which happen from the brainstem (controls involuntary functions such as heart beat and breathing) from progressing to the brain's cortex (controls voluntary activities such as moving about, talking, thinking). The subcortical arousals are important for the baby's survival. The decreased breathing that happens during sleep can make the baby prone to episodes of no breathing or apnoea. The subcortical arousal reestablishes the breathing rhythm with the baby taking shallow rapid breaths. The next in this sequence would be a startle response ('oh-my-God-I-stopped-breathing!' response) and crying for the mother. Swaddling prevents the progression of the arousal from subcortical to cortical and allows the baby to sleep for longer and better.

A word of caution though. Swaddling is not a tight jacket. The baby's blood circulation should not be impaired. The hips and legs should have a little room. The arms need to be swaddled more because the baby's tiny hands can grip a bedding article and cover his face with it. That puts the baby at risk of suffocation. Focus on swaddling the baby's arms snugly and legs with more room for movement.

When not to swaddle?

Swaddling is not absolutely necessary for the baby. If your baby is worse off in the swaddle and valiantly fights for her independence, then do respect her wishes. My daughter hated being swaddled. She had had enough of sleeping in cramped quarters for forty weeks in my womb and refused to have any more of it. She immediately freed herself from the swaddle or cried till we freed her and slept better spread-eagled on me.

Another time you shouldn't swaddle the baby is when he/she is sick

In babies with respiratory infections, give swaddling a skip and rather dress him in comfortable warm clothing. The baby needs to cough or sneeze. Both, cough and sneeze reflex occur by generating adequate pressure in the chest and letting out the irritant in the respiratory tract. It is a protective reflex and helps bring out phlegm or expel the offending pathogen. The pressure exerted by the swaddle will counter the increase of pressure inside the chest and dampen the cough and sneeze reflex.

Sick babies are anyway very clingy to the mother. So, let the baby be on your chest for as long as he wants and continue breastfeeding. Your warmth will regulate his body temperature and give his own heat regulating system a rest. The baby can cough on your chest and your skin will alert your immune system about the germs in your baby's system. Your body will then produce antibodies against the virus/bacteria, and you can feed those antibodies to your baby in your next breastfeeding session.

4

IN BABY'S SICKNESS AND HEALTH

Babies fall sick and that's going to keep happening. As a parent, you need to arm yourself with the knowledge of what to do when and how.

The Misshapen Head Post-delivery

If you have laboured for hours before delivering, chances are the beautiful angel you fantasized about is born with an elongated head. This condition is known as caput succedaneum or caput for short. It seems scary but it is absolutely normal. A baby's skull is designed to pass through the constricting space of the birth canal. The bones are soft and can override each other to squish the skull into a smaller size. Also, there are two empty boneless spots on the skull of the baby which allow the skull bones to overlap during labour. The pressure of the birth canal on the skull causes it to become water-logged and swollen. It is not really a cause of concern and usually resolves within a few days with no intervention. If the child has undergone an instrumental delivery (vacuum or forceps) then the pressure due to the instruments can make the scalp bleed internally. It can result in low blood count and jaundice in the baby and needs close observation by the doctor. It is very rare these days due to increase in caesarean deliveries but it is good to stay informed.

Jaundice

Most newborns have a yellowish tinge to their skin about a day after birth. This is a normal physiological occurrence in babies. When red blood cells (RBCs) die, the end-product is bilirubin. The yellow discoloration of jaundice is caused by it. Newborns have a higher circulating RBC load, which causes more production of bilirubin, and an immature liver that is responsible for its slower elimination.

Depending on the bilirubin levels (assessed by a blood test), the treatment is advised. For bilirubin levels less than 12mg/dl, the baby is advised breastfeeding and sunlight exposure once a day. For higher levels, phototherapy may be required. In this the baby is put in a phototherapy machine which has halogen lights shined on the baby with the baby's eyes and genitals covered. The bilirubin is converted to harmless substances on exposure to this blue light by a process called photo-oxidation. The baby's blood tests maybe done every six–twelve hours depending on the doctor's discretion and often forty-eight hours of phototherapy is all that is needed.

You may come across a term called breastmilk jaundice while Googling jaundice. The existence of this condition can be questioned because:

- There is no sure way of diagnosing it and it is usually a term loosely used in the medical community.
- There are no tests or guidelines to classify the jaundice as breastmilk jaundice or not.
- To treat this kind of jaundice, the mother is often advised to stop breastfeeding for twenty-four hours. Many mothers have suffered an irreversible loss of milk production due to this mindless intervention and the child has not benefited much.
- Even if breastmilk jaundice is a true condition, it is as mild as the physiological jaundice and does not need much intervention.

In fact, breastfeeding should not be stopped if jaundice is diagnosed. The baby should be fed at least eight times a day. The more the baby feeds, the more he will poop and more the bilirubin exits from the body.

If the jaundice occurs before twenty-four hours have passed after birth, it could hint at a liver condition. Long standing jaundice (lasting over two–three weeks) accompanied by pale stools and poor weight gain could be due to pathological jaundice where the cause needs to be investigated. Inherited blood or liver ailments result in pathological jaundice.

Growth

The baby starts to lose weight after his birth and maybe down by about 10 per cent of his birthweight at the end of the first week. This loss is expected as the baby loses water weight. He should ideally start putting back on the lost weight ten days after birth and should exceed his birthweight by day fourteen. If the baby hasn't put back on the weight he lost, then it's not time to start formula, but instead visit a lactation consultant.

In case you have doubts if your baby is well fed, keeping track of wet diapers and the number of stools in a day should alleviate your doubts. Once your milk comes in, the baby will have five–eight wet diapers and three–four stools a day. If the baby sleeps between feeds and seems satisfied for at least an hour after feeds, then you are on the right track. Any doubts about your milk supply should be taken to a lactation consultant and not a drugstore to buy formula milk.

Brain Development

Every experience a newborn goes through contributes to his brain development. The mother's warmth, touch and voice being the major contributors. One important stimulation of the baby is during tummy time. For newborn babies, tummy time can be as short as a minute or two and is best to do it on the mother's chest. Although the baby has very little neck control and may grunt in distress on being made to lie on his tummy, this activity encourages better motor development of the neck muscles and improved eye tracking and understanding. Start with tummy time in the first week after birth and increase the time spent on his tummy from one minute to fifteen minutes two to four times every day over the next few months. Do not put the baby on his tummy when he is sleepy, fussy or right after feeds.

The Constipated Baby

If your baby looks like he is straining to poop, don't immediately jump to conclusions and call up your doctor. Keep an eye on the stools before seeking a solution. That could probably be how he does it. If the baby is formula fed, try to intersperse it with some breastfeeds or water sessions to make up for the fluid deficit. A constipated baby is an unhappy baby and also feeds less as his bowel is loaded.

Some people suggest giving the baby orange juice for constipation. The fibre and fluid is believed to help with the constipation but I would recommend against it for a baby younger than five months old. Early introduction of orange juice to a baby who is formula fed could put the baby at risk for allergy to oranges. The intestines are underdeveloped, and the new food will be presented to the immune system abnormally, sparking an allergic reaction.

Also, avoid giving enemas at home. Many grannies give enemas by introducing a tiny soap or soapy cotton bud up the anus of the baby. It does evacuate the bowels of the baby but also results in copious water loss. The electrolytes lost along with violent bowel evacuation is dangerous for the baby. It is better to visit the doctor and ask for laxatives. If it is only you who is stressed because your baby hasn't done his business in the last few days, then just wait it out.

The Doctor Unapproved: Castor Oil

Castor oil has been a part of raising kids for generations, at times used as punishment and at times remedial. Because of its strong laxative effect adults use it often for relieving constipation but in children it is highly discouraged because of its potential to cause dehydration and electrolyte imbalance by excess motions. A rare condition that can happen in babies due to a high dose of castor oil is intussusception where one part of the intestine goes telescoping into the next.

These cases are few and far in between and babies have been given castor oil for decades. My mother-in-law asked me to give castor oil to my first born but I vehemently refused. She did, however, sneakily give him sometimes when I wasn't around because she was an ardent believer in the oil's goodness. It gives temporary (two–three episodes) loose stools to the baby but does help significantly with constipation.

When my son was three-years-old, he once had a particularly prolonged episode of bronchitis with excess phlegm. Nebulization and syrups had little effect on him. My mother-in-law suggested I give him a tablespoon of castor oil as that would help with clearing up his chest. I was desperate, so I complied. And two loose motions later, his chest miraculously cleared.

I was intrigued by this effect and on digging deeper I came across the active ingredient of castor oil which is ricinoleic acid. Aside from the local effect of causing motions, the ricinoleic acid gets absorbed into the blood stream and can exert its effect on the lungs. And not surprisingly, its effect on the lungs makes it ideal for reducing secretions and congestion. This effect has now found its place as a potential drug treatment in asthmatics.

By the time my daughter was born, I was humbled and not as wary of the effects of castor oil. Since she was a week old, she was given few drops of castor oil every three days and she did just fine. It is believed to help clear out the tarry newborn stools more effectively and help in the baby's gut function. And to my relief, my daughter actually never got a single episode of bronchitis despite always catching her elder brother's virus. It could partly be because she was exclusively breastfed for the longest time and perhaps some of the credit goes to castor oil.

Every medicine has a side effect profile and so does castor oil. Anecdotally, this home remedy has worked wonders for combatting constipation and reducing chest congestion in my son. For newborn babies – few drops suffice, for older babies – half teaspoon after warming (it becomes more fluid on warming and is thicker when at room temperature) and for toddlers over 12 kg, give 1 teaspoon. Warm it a little to bring it to slightly higher than body temperature before giving it to the baby. I cannot prescribe a dose to you weight-wise. So please be careful when giving it to babies. My kids are usually given a dose every two months. Do not give it when the baby is running a fever.

Colic

Babies are fussy. Some babies cry at a certain time of the day everyday till the age of about two–three months. Colic is defined as crying for more than three hours a day, for more than three days a week, for at least three weeks. Even though the cause of colic hasn't been identified, it is more often attributed to tummy problems. Formula-fed babies are often colicky and it could be due to formula milk protein intolerance. Few studies also say it is a form of baby migraine and hence the crying. A stressed mother can cause colic in a baby. If the mother is getting too much grief from someone (say her own mother or mother-in-law) then she needs to take a breather as babies pick up their mother's stress very quickly. Try breathing exercises, listen to some calming music or ask your husband to help out with the baby while you nap. Close body contact with the baby, a firm swaddle, a rocking jholi or a vibrating chair can also help in calming a colicky baby. Evening massage could also be the answer to relieving the colic. Simethicone containing gas drops are often ineffective in relieving colic but can be tried if you feel the baby seems gassy.

If you feel too overwhelmed by the bawling baby, then leave the baby in a safe place and step away from the baby for a few minutes. Do not shake the baby as you might be driven to in a moment of frustration. Shaking can cause internal brain damage or neck injury. Seek help from family and friends. If you have thoughts of harming your child, seek professional help. [For more information on mental health after childbirth please see Chapter 7.]

Spit Up

Some babies are hard to get a burp out of and often spit up. My son was a generous spitter and almost at every feed wasted a lot of my precious milk. Spit up is not a cause of concern like vomiting as it does not dehydrate the baby. The cause of spitting up is that the baby's food pipe is underdeveloped and allows stomach contents to come back up easily. If your baby spits up too much, too often, then these tips should help you:

- Don't lose your mind trying to get a burp out of your baby but do attempt to burp the baby after each feed.
- Try to keep the baby upright for ten–twenty minutes post feed to reduce the amount he spits up. Give head

elevation with a pillow if he has fallen asleep. Night-time feeds are often burpless and it is okay – not worth it to disturb the sleeping baby if the baby is comfortable.

- The consistency of the spit up doesn't matter. If it's curdy then it means the milk had gone further down in the tummy, got partly digested before being brought out.
- Spit up may seem like a lot but the quantity is way less than you can estimate because of how much it spreads on your clothes. As long as the baby is gaining weight and your doctor thinks his growth is all right, then you shouldn't worry.

The Doctor Unapproved: *Kajal*

In India, kajal is often applied to the baby's eyes as early as when the baby is a week old. It is said to protect the baby from the evil eye and also beneficial to the baby's eyes. This custom is centuries old and if you could look beyond the lead poisoning claims of kajal, would you be able to see its benefits? True, there are reports of lead poisoning in little children because of use of inferior-quality-mass-produced kajal, but the kajal used in most Indian homes for babies is made in little quantities from pure ghee. Usually soot collected from burning a wick soaked in ghee is used. In some households, soot from burning garlic is used as the kajal. The minute lead compounds promote production of nitrous oxide which have a beneficial effect on the body's immunity. The astringent properties of kajal protect the baby from seasonal conjunctivitis by reducing inflammation. In earlier times, the kajal was even more important as it protected the eyes from harmful pathogens found in rivers where people often swam and bathed.

Baby's Skin

You might have a small brand-new baby, but his skin comes packed with rather nasty surprises. If your baby has arrived before his due date, then expect a whitish covering on his skin. It protected your baby's skin from the amniotic fluid he had been bouncing in. Babies born close to their due date have mostly shed off their covering and are born with a clear skin.

Another surprise you are likely to encounter at birth or a few days after is milia. Milia are pin head-sized white or skin coloured bumps over your baby's face and neck. If you gently rub your hand over the baby's forehead you will feel the irregularities. It is absolutely normal and a part of the journey your tiny thing goes through before emerging as a beautiful chubby baby. Honestly, a newborn baby isn't one of the prettiest things on the planet but when you are a new mother, you are absolutely in love with your baby. And it is only when you are going through the baby's pictures six months later that you realize you had birthed an alien!

Many babies are born with these bruise-like patches on their legs, buttocks or back. These are the most common spots but can occur elsewhere too. It is called Mongolian spot and there is absolutely nothing you need to do about it. These spots are harmless and reduce in size by the time the kid is four years old. Some might persist well into adulthood. Many mothers worry about this unsightly patch of blue especially in the world where beauty is only skin deep and high premium is placed on the fair and lovely skin. For such mothers I recommend that you should not pay excessive attention to it and to not instil a sense of shame in your child regarding it.

Eczema

Eczema presents as dry scaly patches on the baby's skin. Parts usually affected include cheeks, areas around the wrist and shins. It is not exactly due to allergy, but allergic kids do have eczema quite commonly. It is often a fleeting episode and goes away on its own if the skin is moisturized well. In some children it could be due to the introduction of formula milk.

Some tips to soothe an eczema attack:

1. Avoid using very hot water for baths. It is quite common to use hot water to bathe the baby as it is quite sedating. Use warm water for bathing the baby instead.
2. Use of olive oil and some herbal preparations are usually fine but can further damage the already damaged skin. Avoid these oils in affected areas.
3. The most popular baby soaps are heavily perfumed. Avoid these. You might have got big fat hampers from your visitors which have baby powder, soaps, lotions and oils. Do not get happy that you are loaded with a year's

supply of toiletries and open them. Pass them on to other new mommies! (Cheap, I know, but you'll totally get me when you are a mother.)

4. Moisturize when the skin is damp. Following this tip really helped me with my son's brief stint of eczema. Moisturize the baby with a generous slather of a deep moisturizing lotion (again dermatologist recommended) within three minutes of his bath. It's a real game changer for skin with eczema.
5. The best regimen for looking after eczema is putting a mixture of pure, non-perfumed petroleum jelly such as Vaseline and pure coconut oil (commonly used coconut hair oil is usually perfumed, so be cautious). Mix both ingredients in equal proportions and apply to the baby's skin after bath and at night. The petroleum jelly serves as an excellent carrier for the soothing coconut oil and poses a barrier to water loss from the damaged skin.

Tonsuring and Cradle Cap

Shaving the baby's head or tonsuring is an important custom all over India. Among Muslims, the baby is tonsured on the 7th day of life, an animal is slaughtered, and a feast is thrown. The child's name is announced publicly. This naming-cum-tonsuring ceremony is known as *Aqeeqah*. In Hindus, the tonsuring ceremony is often delayed to the first or second birthday as they believe the hair protects the baby's head's soft spot and should not be removed.

However, early hair removal also has its advantages. Infants of up to three months often suffer from scalp infection or cradle cap. The fungus Malassezia is one of the culprits causing the skin damage leading to cradle cap. Tonsuring removes this fungus which often resides in the baby's hair and also exposes the scalp so that the mother can easily detect the dermatitis before it spreads.

The incidence of cradle cap has increased in recent times thanks to the rising number of caesarean deliveries. When the baby passes through the birth canal during normal delivery, he ends up swallowing the good bacteria, lactobacillus, that reside in the vaginal walls. This bacterium has a protective role against the Malassezia fungus. (One aspect of treatment of cradle cap in adults these days is supplementing with the lactobacillus probiotic.) The immobility of the newborn also predisposes him to this skin condition. Daily massage improves blood circulation and offers a degree of protection against it.

Cradle cap presents as oily yet scaly skin patches. It looks sort of like dandruff or just scum. You will be tempted to peel off the scales but refrain from doing so. It is thought to be partly due to overproduction of oil by the baby's oil glands and partly because of the Malassezia fungus.

1. Your doctor will prescribe a medicated shampoo/cleanser
2. After bath, when the head is still damp, you can use a soft bristled brush to remove the scales off the baby's

scalp. Or instead use it during the bath time and you can wash away the scales.

3. Same as eczema, the skin here is damaged and inflamed so avoid the use of olive oil or any other baby oil on the affected areas. Although, you can use moisturizers on the affected part.

Diaper Rash

For a redness in the nappy area, use coconut oil and leave the baby diaper free for a couple of hours to let him heal. If that isn't feasible, then use a diaper cream that contains ingredients such as zinc oxide and benzyl alcohol as these are the most effective for treating rashes. Even ghee works wonders as a diaper cream. Do not use rash creams regularly while diapering if there is no rash.

Oral thrush and fungal diaper rashes

Oral thrush is caused by the fungus Candida albicans and commonly infects babies. It is not particularly a cause for concern but in breastfed babies it can cause the mother to get infection of the nipple which is rather painful. And if the baby and mother aren't simultaneously treated, then they can keep passing the infection back and forth. Babies who had a course of antibiotics are more prone to it as the good bacteria residing in the mouth get killed too and the fungus can grow freely. If the mother has had a course of antibiotics, then the baby gets affected as well. Bottle-fed babies and babies who sleep with pacifiers in their mouths are more prone to it because the teat serves as a carrier of fungus.

Thrush is a white patch on the tongue which bleeds or looks raw when you try to wipe it clean. It has a curdy appearance usually when present on the tongue. Sometimes there are accompanying white patches on the inner surface of the lips and cheeks too. Do not go about suspecting fungal infection each time you see your baby's tongue looking white. Quite often, it is just milk residue. If in doubt, it is better to have it examined by your doctor.

This infection is not caused due to negligence. So, there is no sure shot way to avoid it but if your baby is on pacifier then be sure to remove it from his mouth when he dozes off. Do sterilize bottles and pacifiers daily in hot water.

Treatment:

An antifungal mouth paint (commonly cotrimazole) is given. Apply the liquid using a clean cotton bud on the affected areas of the baby's mouth and your nipples after feeds. There is no need to wash off from nipples before the next feed.

One of the side effects of having oral thrush is a fungal diaper rash. The fungus passes through the digestive tract and affects the skin of the diaper area. If a diaper rash is not responding to your regular diaper rash cream and seems to be growing, then suspect a fungal infection. Be sure to get it diagnosed correctly by your paediatrician.

Treatment:

1. Apply cotrimazole cream on the affected areas twice a day. At other times use regular nappy creams.
2. Make the baby sit in a potassium permanganate bath, with the bum soaking in it, once a day for five minutes, It works wonders.

Fever

These days it is being increasingly recognized that fever has a major protective role during infections and should not be reduced indiscriminately. However, fever in a baby less than three months old, if not following a vaccination, should be immediately seen by your doctor. Babies have a very immature immune system and the cause of the fever should be treated promptly. The doctor may need to run some tests too before starting treatment. Irrespective of fever, if the baby is dull, irritable or refusing feeds, then that also warrants medical attention. For older children, a wait and watch policy can be adopted. You can wait two–three days before seeing your paediatrician if the child doesn't look too ill or if the baby's temperature (armpit) is below 101°F. Fever control is by paracetamol drops and the dosage should be given based on weight and not age (most drops have doses written on the leaflet based on age. Do not follow that). Seizures due to fever are not seen in children below the age of six months. If the fever is accompanied by a new rash or the child has a chronic medical problem, then do get him checked by the doctor. Do not stop breastfeeding the baby in case of a fever.

Vaccination

The vaccine debate has been an unnecessary and futile exercise which has left parents undecided and kids suffering due to their indecision. Some diseases are argued to be better off not prevented such as chicken pox, as the protection offered by the vaccination wanes after around a decade whereas immunity gained by natural infection is lifelong. Adults are more prone to getting chicken pox if they have been vaccinated as kids (and it's more severe if you get it as a grown up). So, am I saying it is better not to vaccinate? Of course not. Vaccine schedules need to be made for adults too so that their immunity from childhood vaccination is boosted well into adulthood.

It's not all gloom and doom if your child is not vaccinated, parents argue. Would he get the infection for sure? Most likely not, because the infection isn't actively circulating in the community. Or so you thought.

Measles was declared eliminated in USA in 2000 because of vaccination efforts. However, soon after the anti-vaccination campaign begun in 1998, linking autism to the MMR vaccine, the number of parents vaccinating their children declined. The study was faultily designed and had some of the data fabricated. The study has since then been discredited and withdrawn, and the scientist's medical licence was also revoked but by then the damage had been done. Hordes of parents continue to choose to not vaccinate their kids. And the efforts of the medical community continue to be wasted trying to educate anti-vaxxers. Resources are also wasted in debunking the link between autism and MMR rather than researching the cause of autism.

At this point, I want to introduce you to herd immunity. This is the protection vaccination offers to unprotected individuals (too young, too old or those with low immunity) when a majority of the population is vaccinated. Mass vaccination protects the entire population from the infection. Even if someone catches the infection, the disease does not spread to the vaccinated children and the chain of transmission is interrupted. When more parents choose not to vaccinate, the infection can spread unchecked and children suffer because of a disease that could have been completely avoided. The number of outbreaks reported in the US are because of travellers bringing in the infection from other countries and the virus spreading unchecked to the unvaccinated children. So, please vaccinate your child!

Post-vaccine care

The baby could get a fever after vaccination and may feed less. That is because a milder form of the disease is introduced into the body and an immune response is being mounted against it. For a baby less than twelve weeks old, fever needs medical attention. If the spot is sore, some cold sponging on the spot will ease the pain. Seek immediate medical help if the child is crying at a high pitch for over one hour or has been persistently crying for over three hours.

Respiratory Infections

One of the most common infections in early childhood, that no amount of immunity or vaccination can prevent, is the common cold. A tiny infant, especially, is particularly distressed by a blocked nose. The baby has difficulty nursing and very little babies cannot breathe through the mouth in case of a nose block.

One of my relatives swears by ajwain leaf as the best remedy for cold and I agree with her passion towards this leaf. Hold the fresh leaf on a flame till it wilts to a dark green colour. Apply massage oil on the soft spot of the baby's head, place the wilted leaf on it and cover his head with a cap. It sounded pretty voodoo-ish and funny to me but no harm in giving it a try. I did not wish to give such a small baby cold medicine as yet. I relied on nasal saline drops and the ajwain leaf magic to get her through her cold and her cold was mild and lasted for just three days.

For future episodes of colds, I gave my daughter ajwain leaf juice when she was slightly older. And it worked great for her. Cold medicines dry up the secretions and increase the nose block severity. The baby often develops dry cough after recovering from the cold. And the more I researched for this book, the more I moved away from contemporary medicine towards nature to look for home remedies that actually worked. Ajwain happens to be one of the best remedies for the common cold for little children as well as adults.

For babies less than four months:

Hold the leaf over a flame till it turns dark green. Don't let it get charred. Place on the soft spot of baby's head with baby's regular massage oil and cover the head with a cap.

OR

Grind ajwain seeds to a very fine powder. Apply the powder on baby's chest.

OR

Make a small *potli* (pouch) of roasted ajwain seeds. Use a clean handkerchief to make the potli. Take 1 tsp salt and 1 tsp ajwain seeds and roast on a pan. Put in the handkerchief and tie a knot with the corners of the handkerchief. Place the warm potli on the baby's chest. (Make sure the potli isn't too hot.)

For babies older than four months:

Hold the ajwain (Indian Borage) leaf over a flame and wilt it to a dark green colour. Remove the leaf in a bowl and allow it to cool (usually takes fifteen–thirty seconds to cool). Squeeze the wilted leaves to yield the juice. Feed the juice to the baby with a clean spoon.

This remedy is most effective when the baby starts showing signs of catching a cold. It diminishes the course of the cold and reduces the likelihood of developing a blocked nose.

Give 1 tsp of the juice to the baby. Ideally one hour before sleep. You can give upto two–three times a day. And depending on the thickness and size of the leaf, you can get 1 tsp juice from just once thick juicy leaf or might need three–four leaves for the same yield if the leaves are small.

A cold can be terrible for breastfeeding mothers. With the baby next to you, it is hard to blow your nose without disturbing the baby's sleep. And when all you wanted to do is sleep when the baby sleeps, your dry hacking cough will jolt him awake! A new mother's immunity is also low for the first two–three months after delivery, so she is particularly susceptible to colds. Ajwain leaves work just as well for the sniffles in the mother.

Just like I mentioned for the baby, you can wilt the leaves over a flame. For grownups, chewing three–four leaves is fine. Put a pinch of salt on the leaves and roll it up and chew the leaf just like a paan. It has a mildly bitter taste but nothing you cannot stomach. The minute you feel like you have the beginnings of a scratchy throat, reach out for your ajwain paan! It will nip the infection in the bud.

If you know someone who is pregnant or just had a baby, gift her a pot of ajwain plant for her baby shower!

Ajwain is better than over-the-counter cold medicines as it does not dry up secretions. Ajwain has an antibacterial effect preventing a viral infection from getting superimposed by a bacterial one. It also reduces secretions and clears up congestion. It works best if given when the infection is just beginning and thwarts the course of the cold.

Nebulization

Many parents have asked me if steam is the same as nebulization. In fact, because of the vapours, parents assume it is the same thing. Well it is not, neither in composition nor in function.

1. Nebulization is deposition of a drug into the airways. A fine mist is produced by the nebulizer and when inhaled with a mask, gets delivered to the smaller airways and lungs.

   Steam is warm water vapour for humidifying sinuses and airways. No drug is deposited. It just prevents drying of the airways and makes the secretions moist and easy to clear.
2. Nebulization is used for chest congestion and bronchitis. Steam is used for sinus congestion and nose blocks.
3. Nebulization uses bronchodilator drugs. The effect is reduction of inflammation of the airways, controlling the hypersecretion of mucus in the lungs and consequently opening up of smaller air passages.
4. Nebulization is not very safe. The drug is delivered at a high pressure to the airways and the baby has to bear a strong positive pressure on its lungs. A doctor,

after examination, will assess the need for such an intervention. Parents should refrain from giving their children nebulization without getting their paediatrician's opinion.

Ear Infections

The baby will be very fussy and wailing non-stop when he/she gets affected by a middle ear infection. The baby generally would have had a cold for the past few days which would have progressed to an ear infection. A parent should suspect an ear infection if the baby is tugging the ear while crying. A dose of decongestant cold medicine and a regular paediatric paracetamol/ibuprofen often takes care of the immediate crisis till you can schedule a paediatrician appointment. On examination, the doctor will see a grossly retracted or an angry, inflamed ear drum. The baby will be advised nose drops, decongestants and a painkiller. Antibiotics should *not* be routinely prescribed for every ear infection. If the child's condition doesn't seem to improve in 48 hours and there is a spiking fever with chills, then the use of antibiotics is justified. Nowadays, there is a push towards using locally acting pain medicine such as anaesthetic ear drops or natural substitutes such as a garlic infused oil. Oral pain medicine brings down the fever too but rigorous control of fever is discouraged as it helps in combating infection.

Often a well-meaning neighbour will pop by with a ready diagnosis and a prescription before you have zeroed down on the ear infection as the source of your baby's misery. Experienced probably with ear infection in her own child, she will ask you to give these ear drops to the baby which apparently worked wonders for her own child. Please – never ever give ear drops to your baby without the doctor's prescription! The ear drum which is inflamed can get perforated (burst open) because of the infection building pressure in the middle ear. Putting ear drops will not limit its effect in the external ear canal but also find its way into the middle ear through the hole in the ear drum. The antibiotic in the ear drops frequently sold at the pharmacy, are ototoxic (unsafe for the nerves in ear) and can cause hearing impairment in your child. And most of these ear drops are such a cocktail of medicines. They include a pain killer, a steroid, anti-bacterial and anti-fungal in one medication. It is such a blanket approach to the problem that I am surprised it is even manufactured by pharmaceutical companies so shamelessly. The eardrum perforation is often pin hole-sized and can self heal over time, but ear drops usage in such a child is a gross negligence on the part of the parent.

Infection in the external ear canal

The part of the ear which you can see is the external ear canal. Sometimes babies vigorously scratch their ears because they are sleepy or just for the heck of it. The scratches can become infected and cause a painful condition called otitis externa. There can be pus discharge or little bleeding from the ear of an inconsolable baby. The diagnosis is fairly simple. If the pain is severe then your doctor will insert a wick into the baby's ear. It is a long cotton wick dipped in painkillers and inserted into the ear canal to reduce pain and inflammation. Ear drops or locally applied antibiotic creams should suffice for treating the infection. If the infection is accompanied by a middle ear infection, then both need to be treated as per the principles I outlined in the previous section.

The Umbilical Stump

Normally the umbilical cord stump falls out anywhere between the day four and day ten after birth. The advice given on care of the cord can range from do absolutely nothing to something as bizarre as applying cow dung on the stump. The umbilical stump is an unhealed wound and is susceptible to infections if meddled with too much. Scientists are still scratching their heads when it comes to standardizing the care of the cord. The latest guidelines of swabbing with sterile alcohol wipes have been changed to leave the cord to air dry but you cannot leave your baby exposed to air all day long. You need to bathe him and swaddle him and breastfeed him while also taking care that the cord stays infection and friction free. In this section I will explore common cord care practices.

In some developing countries, the cord is cut by the mother, preferably and often with an unhygienic blade. In addition, application of mother's saliva, mustard oil, not maintaining hand hygiene while handling the baby results in an infection of the umbilical stump. The infection can be dangerous if left untreated and spread to the entire skin of the abdomen. While it has been proven beyond doubt that unclean cord care and lack of hand hygiene causes infections in the baby, the effects of pouring mustard oil on the stump are yet to be researched.

On the other hand, while educating mothers on the importance of clean cord care, health workers advise mothers to use antiseptics to keep the cord infection free. Use of antiseptic lowered the rate of infections but delayed the dropping of the cord. This delay is worrisome in many families. Use of betadine, alcohol swabs and antiseptics on any wound delays healing by killing the healthy multiplying cells.

What I recommend:

In India, while massaging the baby, oil is poured generously around the umbilical stump area without touching the stump. The baby is lathered with ubtan and a warm water bath is given. In the first ten days the baby's bath water is prepared by boiling neem leaves in water. The stump is gently patted dry. Friction and tugging from clothes can result in traction on the stump causing a red fleshy scar to appear. It is advised to loosely tie the nappy and include the stump in it. Swaddle the baby snugly and friction will be less while handling the baby. This is the exact care both my babies were given.

Multiple pathways in wound healing are benefited from the application of pure coconut oil as evidenced by higher collagen cross linking, increased fibroblast proliferation and neovascularizaton. These fancy medical terms basically mean that things that are supposed to be happening in a healing tissue at the microscopic level are happening in full swing because of the coconutty goodness. The use of neem in bath water prevents infection in the stump. Neem extract stops bacteria from clinging onto the healing surface rather than mindlessly killing healthy cells along with the bacteria as is the case with antibiotics and antiseptics.

Another practice in cord care seen in Asian countries is pouring a few drops of mother's milk on the stump. Studies have also shown that application of a few drops of the mother's milk twice a day has a beneficial effect on the stump and does not delay cord falling the way antiseptics do. After the baby's bath, you can express some of your milk and apply few drops. Do make sure your hands are clean while applying the milk.

Mothers are usually worried while diapering a baby with umbilical stumps. Many suggest folding the top part of the diaper to avoid contact with the stump. In my experience that exposes the stump to friction from the baby's clothing. A better alternative would be to loosely secure the diaper over the stump. Change the diaper more frequently to ensure that the urine from a wet diaper doesn't come in contact with the stump.

In case of umbilical trouble

A non-healing or draining umbilical stump beyond two weeks needs medical attention to assess for infection or a malformation that needs surgical treatment. Your surgeon may require an ultrasound for confirming the diagnosis.

In case the cord gets tugged at any time during or after delivery, it could result in a fleshy red scar tissue instead of a tiny navel. When left untreated it can progress to become an unsightly outie belly button as an adult or get badly infected with drainage of greenish discharge for days till it is not treated (see above for management of discharge from the stump).

The often-recommended line of treatment is chemical cauterization of the tissue with the chemical silver nitrate. It is effective but if the chemical touches the unaffected area it can cause a burn on the baby's skin. Steroid application is also recommended medically but it can cause skin thinning. A simple remedy is applying cooking salt to the tissue and is now recommended from good old Asian wisdom. Sprinkle some common salt on it and leave it on for thirty minutes. Then, wash it off. For best results you need to apply twice a day for five–seven days.

Another simple tip to tackle this condition is the coin method. Take a coin and wrap it in a cloth. Place the covered coin on the tissue and tie a band of cloth encircling the baby's abdomen to hold the coin in place. The ties which come with the swaddling sets can be used for the purpose of securing the coin on the navel. Even if the stump has fallen off leaving a healthy belly button in its place, the coin application is advised for a day or two. The pressure application can be done after bathtime till the next diaper change.

Circumcision

Circumcision is snipping the foreskin of the penis for religious reasons or as a personal preference. From a medical perspective, it is favoured but not recommended to everyone because of better hygiene and protection against penile cancer in the future. Penis hygiene can be maintained well in non-circumcised males too. So, it is more a matter of personal choice in today's age.

Although many families have their child's circumcision performed by a surgeon, there are still some who get it done by a trained religious person. There are some conditions wherein circumcision should not be done. If the child has a urinary opening on the upper (epispadias) or lower (hypospadias) surface of the penis, then the foreskin should be left intact. The skin can be used in the repositioning surgery of urinary opening which is usually performed at the age of one year. Get your baby examined by a doctor to get approval for circumcision and rule out any such condition.

The ideal age to perform circumcision would be under the age of one. It can be performed with local anaesthesia and the child will have a lower awareness of the procedure. In my opinion, once the child's umbilical stump falls off, you can get him circumcised (one less wound to care for). Anywhere between two weeks of age to three months is good as a child this small does not roll over or kick his legs. A child who can roll over needs to be supervised and taken care of more after the surgery. A smaller baby cannot reach the operated area with his hands either so that is also advantageous. Such small children have a rapid recovery time, are less fussy than older kids and easier to manage as they mostly lie on their backs.

Care of the circumcised baby

It takes about five–seven days for a scab to appear and fall off from the circumcised area. The surgeon will use a local anaesthesia and operate on the baby and the whole procedure lasts about ten minutes. Be prepared with some honey or paracetamol syrup before the surgery so that you can give the baby pain relief as soon as he is out of the operating room. Some children don't require the painkiller and are content with only being breastfed. The first two days when the area is raw, use an antibiotic ointment to keep the area infection free. I would advise that you keep the baby diaper free in the first two days at least for the area to heal but in case it is too cold, or you cannot keep up with him peeing all over the place then use a diaper which is two sizes bigger so that it does not touch the penis tip.

Do not bathe the baby till the wound has completely healed. Sponge bathing should suffice. Once the scab starts to form you can use a dusting antibiotic or antiseptic powder to keep the area infection free. Apply the ointment/powder not more than three times a day.

5 BREASTFEEDING

We all know breastfeeding is best but something so natural does not come naturally to all mothers. It takes days of practice, a lot of pain and tears and a ton of encouragement to be able to breastfeed your baby like a pro. With rising breastfeeding awareness more mothers are opting for it, but it is not an easy path to tread. And for moms who haven't been able to exclusively breastfeed for whatever reason, there is always a second chance. I had my share of struggles with my firstborn and had to resort to topping his feeds with formula. And I have lived with guilt to this day for not being a good enough mother. I am writing this chapter for the mothers battling with guilt, dilemmas or just struggling to take care of their little ones. I know the pain a mother goes through trying to feed her milk to her precious child.

Know the Basics

The human body is very smart. Our body has an awesomely regulated system that ensures the use of its precious resources (that's why it's so hard to lose weight!). The human milk is nutrient-dense and tailor-made for the developing baby. A lot of energy, food and if I may add, love, goes into making it. And if you thought breastmilk comes gushing when the baby is born, you are far from the truth. Just like in the marketplace, the supply will only come when there is demand. A baby needs to suck quite a bit for the mother's milk to be produced.

The first three–four days of the infant's life are for dry sucking. The milk will be a few drops only and that is perfectly fine at first. There is no such thing as a mother not making milk. Failure of lactation is not because of low milk production or malfunctioning breasts. What usually leads to failure is the mother not getting support, guidance, and encouragement from the people who were there to look after her. Just because your breasts are not engorged, leaking or gushing with milk in the first few days does not mean you will not make enough milk. It could take a week before the milk production finally picks up.

However, when your newborn sucks for three hours straight at each feed and cries even after that, all your Googled knowledge as well as confidence goes right out of the window. With my son, what started off as confusion as to why he wouldn't stop sucking, went on to become a sense of helplessness and failure. Babies need to suck a lot to establish a good milk flow. And many mothers will be saved a lot of misery and self-doubt if the people surrounding her knew and believed that. The matriarch breathing down her neck watching her breasts 'not produce enough milk' has clearly forgotten her own struggles as a new mom. She often projects herself as a fountain of motherhood with milk and love oozing out of every pore. She laments how, *aaj kal ki ladkiyan bachon ko doodh nahi pilati* (girls don't want to breastfeed these days) but it is the mother, mother-in-law and the overbearing aunt whose taunts belittle the breasts and baby-rearing skills of the *aaj kal ki ladki*. All this nay-saying and booing is what is drying up the milk. Performance anxiety has a strong negative impact on the mother's psychological state and therefore, on the milk let-down reflex. The mother, the breast and the baby would live in perfect harmony if not for the taunts and the jibes she is often subjected to.

The milk machine

During pregnancy, the breasts enlarge and get prepped up due to the effect of oestrogen and progesterone. Oestrogen causes the milk ducts to develop whereas progesterone promotes the growth of the milk-producing sacs called Acini. One important hormone responsible for milk production is Prolactin. Progesterone opposes the action of prolactin's milk-producing effect on the breast during pregnancy. And thank God for that! Otherwise we would be leaking on our shirts throughout the nine months. The hormone responsible for the milk to flow into the baby's mouth is oxytocin. Each time the baby sucks, oxytocin is released in your brain. Under its effect, milk is ejected and the uterus contracts. You will feel a gush of blood in your maxi pad every time your baby starts to suck. Be prepared to expect this perfectly normal yet supremely irritating phenomenon for the first couple of days.

The first milk: Colostrum

Colostrum is the first milk that comes out. It is a yellowish white milk rich in antibodies and nutrients. The antibodies present in the colostrum coat the delicate developing intestines of the newborn, giving him a head start in his lifelong battle against germs and diseases but sadly, many from the granny generation believe that the initial milk is a waste and should not be fed to the baby. They could not have been more wrong. In fact, I have even heard many supposedly well-meaning nanis and dadis say that water should be given sparingly to the new mother as it dilutes her milk. I'd like to observe a moment of silence for this outrageous idiocy. I have had patients develop constipation and piles after their delivery because of this water restriction.

The monster latch

Most newborns want to just latch onto their mothers like there is no tomorrow. This latch is non-nutritive and for comfort. The baby is basically using mommy as a pacifier. It is exhausting for the mother, not to mention painful, if the excessive sucking has caused nipple soreness (as is the case mostly). One important thing that a new mother needs to remember is that the baby lived nine months inside her. It was living at the right temperature and was always surrounded by the soothing voice of the mother, the whoosh whoosh of the blood in her arteries, the blurp blurp of the gut, the steady pace of air filling in and emptying out of the lungs and a perpetual supply of glucose. The baby's room was dark and cosy. He/she was buoyant in his/her amniotic sea and happily bouncing, kicking, twisting and somersaulting in merry slow motion in muffled gravity. Voices of the real world reached the baby in bits and bobs in this paradise. Baby felt no cold, mom was always around and food was never scant. And one day the world of a newborn is suddenly turned upside down on being birthed. But this innocent little child still recognizes his/her mother by her scent and voice. The breast and amniotic fluid have a similar smell and babies promptly make the connection and go for the mother's breast. The nipple is like the baby's lifeboat and he/she doesn't want to let go. That is the only way he/she can re-establish connection with the nurturer. This scared little baby sucks all day and all night in order to feel reassured that the fount of bounty is going to be around and will take care of him/her.

Another thing to bear in mind is that this child is unfamiliar to the concept of hunger. The baby is used to a steady supply of glucose from the mother throughout his/her life in the womb. Even if the mother is hungry, the body manufactures ketone bodies by breaking down fat to nourish the child. For the newborn, hunger is a cruel introduction to the real world. Only after a few weeks will the baby begin to learn that feeding does not need to be round the clock. And that when out of sight, mommy will be back as soon as the baby cries bringing along her delicious goodness.

Many new mothers have suffered and continue to suffer because neither their doctors/relatives/partners know of this concept of latching for comfort or dry sucking. *The baby sucks not only when he/she is hungry but also for comfort, warmth and even for entertainment.* In fact, newborns think sucking is the answer to everything. For instance, my daughter, on feeling uncomfortable due to overfeeding, would suck even more. According to her little baby logic, sucking on mumma solved all problems. The additional sucking would make her tummy fuller and leave her all the more restless. At the end of half hour when she would be chomping at my nipple with more vigour, that would be my cue to make her unlatch and comfort her.

One of my patients had the problem of her first born sucking all day long. She was swiftly labelled as not producing enough milk by her own mother and aunt. Formula milk was not common in rural Kerala, so it was not given to her allegedly 'starving' infant. The matriarchs pressured that poor mother into starting top feeds for the baby and unfortunately, it did not come out of a milk bottle. It was a special variety of local banana used for weaning older babies. A great weaning food for a six-month-old, but a terrible choice for a new born. The underdeveloped gut of the baby was subjected to this cruelty that was the banana. The next day the baby developed violent loose stools, bloating and gas. The grannies had to compromise and allow formula feeding because nothing trumps the point a wailing newborn makes! In her heart my patient knew she could have fed her son had it not been for the opposition her breastfeeding faced. All she needed was less meddling and more time for adjustment. However, the story has a happy ending. When she returned to Bangalore to live with her baby and husband, she gradually phased out the bottle one feed at a time and in a matter of a week, managed to exclusively breastfeed her little one.

I too have had my share of discouragement and formula promotion when I struggled with initiating breastfeeding for my firstborn.

Preparing for Breastfeeding

Any bra can be a nursing bra if you choose to nurse in it. It is difficult to go bra shopping after the baby is born and online shopping just doesn't cut it because you don't get to try it on. A nursing bra, in my opinion, is not necessary. It's just a bra that opens out at the nipple region. After a few weeks of practice at nursing and once your ballooned breasts shrink a bit, you will find that lifting your bra does the trick. In fact, special front opening nursing shirts sold in the maternity clothes section will just pinch your pocket and not do anything else.

The perfect fit

A simple supportive bra with no underwires works well for a nursing mother. Go shopping for a bra that fits well at the tightest clasp in your second trimester. The cup size increases only slightly once your baby is born and many women can comfortably wear the same pregnancy bras during nursing. You can use a padded bra to prevent your nipples from peeking through your top. A padded bra also offers an extra layer to soak up any milk leaks without staining your shirt. Nonetheless, reserve those for outings and at home opt for simple bras with breast pads for better hygiene.

You don't need to unhook your bra at each feed. Just lift off the cup to expose the breast and you are good to go. Unhooking and hooking back on, multiple times a day for breastfeeding, will cause the area next to the clasp (where you dig your thumbs to get a grip on the bra) to wear out. This is something that moms don't talk about but have faced – bras with thumb shaped holes adjacent to the clasp!

A loose, breathable top is your go to breastfeeding dress code. Even feeding in public can be achieved wearing such a top. The upper portion of the breast is covered by the kurta/shirt. The nipple is in the baby's mouth and the lower portion of the breast is covered by the baby's head. You don't need any shawl or covers to hide what you're doing. You can nurse in plain sight without revealing anything besides the fact that you are breastfeeding.

Breast pads

This is a necessity in the first one or two months of nursing. Once the milk supply gets fairly adjusted to the baby's hunger your leakage episodes will stop too. Up till then you will need lots of breast pads to soak up the leaks. I do not recommend buying disposable breast pads unless you need to go out in public. Aside from the convenience of being disposable, they don't have much to offer. A simple soft cotton wash cloth works great. Be sure to wash and dry them regularly to prevent irritation and infection.

Front-open button-down nightie

At night, sleep braless to let your breasts breathe and the circulation pick up. Breastfeeding night gowns are wasteful just like nursing bras. They are not as comfortable as one would hope for them to be and the open zipper causes irritation to the baby's delicate face. Also, wear a button-down nightie that opens in the front. An experienced mother will tell you how the baby basically sleeps between her breasts during the night. Latching when he/she wants to and drinking to his/her heart's content. In fact, most mothers can vouch for the fact that they are unaware of how many times their baby is feeding at night. The mother and baby groggily reach out for each other at meal times and the baby feeds happily with neither of them needing to wake completely.

Saboteurs and Self-doubters

The entire society and healthcare system are responsible for successful breastfeeding. The reality is, however, very different. Doctors are scarcely sensitized to supporting breastfeeding, formula companies have a strong lobby and matriarchs quite often look disapprovingly at the fumbling mother. Let us look at some of these protagonists who are meant to support but instead end up sabotaging successful breastfeeding.

The support system at home

My book is not intended to bash the mother-in-law. Many women I know have perfectly lovable mothers-in-law, so do I. But the unfiltered truth is that many have hostile territorial moms, or a know-it-all mother-in-law or an always-right aunt. Some women are lucky to have a solid support system in place and can expect food, guidance and help while taking care of their newborns. Unfortunately, though, more than one has ended up suffering because of their 'supporters' rather than reap the benefits of extra helping hands.

Saboteur #1: Much ado about the leaky breast

A friend of mine told me about her pestering mother-in-law who interfered a lot with her breastfeeding. She would often inspect her daughter-in-law's nipples and rudely even press the nipple to express milk and see if the daughter-in-law was making milk worthy of her precious grandson. As meddlesome as she was, the daughter-in-law managed to block her interference out and do her thing. The mother-in-law would often boast how her breasts were always overflowing with milk when she fed her son. And how she would leak from one side while she fed her baby from the other side.

First things first. The mother-in-law is very intrusive and needs to respect the new mother's personal space. Secondly, the mother-in-law has tweaked the memory of leaky breasts of the first few weeks (or maybe even months if she was an over producer) into a two-year long festival of milk extravaganza. Breasts are smart and perfect and aren't wasteful faucets. Some mothers have a gushing supply and some mothers have inconspicuous leaks for the first few weeks. A few mothers have faced the issue of over production and have a more rapid let-down than others, like perhaps this mother-in-law, but it's a temporary phase in all mothers.

Many well meaning matriarchs have declared the new moms as having insufficient milk and at best requested (read: nag) them to start formula, or at worst, compelled them. This is one of the most rampant acts of sabotage I have come across. It is just a made-up claim of low milk production. Squirting, leaking or gushing milk is not a sign of ample milk supply. It is a sign of the initial adjustment while building a milk supply. Some breasts leak more than others, and some make milk adequately without much wastage. It is the second category that is nagged into the zone of self-doubt.

On the contrary, the formula supplementation ends up setting off the vicious cycle of low demand at the breast by baby and subsequent low supply. What started as topping a breastfeed then turns into a necessity for the baby. The mother's breastmilk production scales back to meet the lower demand for breastmilk. And often the mother cannot recover from this setback.

Saboteur #2: Why is she pressing my buttons?

Aastha wrote to me:

> My mother-in-law keeps saying 'your milk isn't enough for the baby'. When I switch sides during a feed my mother-in-law watches and comments 'when my son was a baby and I would change sides, his face would be showered by my milk by the time he latched on'. Apart from her imaginary assessment of my 'low milk', there is absolutely no indicator that the baby isn't getting enough milk. He is happy when fed and doesn't demand till two–three hours. She is also asking me to start formula and get the baby used to the bottle. How do I handle her?

This patient of mine knew her milk was enough. She was well-read and knew the basics of breastfeeding rather well and had a strong network of friends who themselves were breastfeeding moms, but handling a mother-in-law's taunts is not something you can learn from anywhere. Most of us have to suffer at the hands of an insufferable matriarch. A daughter-in-law and mother-in-law might have been getting along splendidly before the delivery but once the baby is born, there is a perceptible shift from the nice, progressive mother-in-law to a territorial know-it-all grandmother.

Taking care of a baby is a huge task and comes with little training. A new mom makes a few mistakes before figuring out how to change a diaper with a surgeon's skill and how to breastfeed in her sleep but the grandmother often has zero chill and wants everything to be perfect in the first go. What she needs to realize is that once upon a time she too was a fumbling mother and that she too got the hang of keeping a baby alive only after a period of time. I can break down the behaviour into the following analysis and you can read, ruminate and recognize what exactly is your matriarch's problem. Please remember one thing though – we cannot change anyone. This section is to help you accept that controlling person in your life. Maybe forgive her and make your life a little lighter and easier to lead once you let go a little bit.

a. *The illusion of control*

A matriarch is used to being a mother all her life. It is what she does best. It's a force of habit to want to feel needed. Be a little sympathetic to her. Once the baby is born, she genuinely sees her own flesh and blood in an extremely dependent form. It's a beautiful tiny baby. And nothing is more of a beacon of hope than a baby.

The maternal figure, however, needs to realize that she only plays the supporting role. The new mother is the heroine of this drama and the mother-in-law must let her lead the show. If she needs help, give it to her. It is very difficult for grandmothers to understand and grasp that. They think they know best. And maybe they actually do but that does not give them the right to deem the intelligence and intuition of the new mother as garbage. Everyone has brains, and nothing ever good comes out of underestimating someone's intelligence and expertise.

The grandchild is basically her own. And controlling the new mother makes her the master controller. If you look back in history, most of the elements of patriarchy and misogyny have one common root – *control of the uterus.* Curbing a woman's right to work, vote or rule. Curbing a woman's sexuality, right to birth control, honour killing, female foeticide, dowry. Even little things like men eating before the women stem from misogyny. All are linked to having the reins of fertility and child bearing in the hands of the men. Imagine a world where women ruled and controlled it all. Men would become highly dispensable except for their one sperm. If you control the uterus, you control the entire generation.

At some level, all of us Indians have ingrained misogyny in us. It is just how we were raised. We are getting more and more progressive, but we still have a long way to go. One of the manifestations of deep-rooted patriarchy is saying the mother is not good enough. And who is better at belittling a woman than another woman?

As a daughter-in-law, there is nothing much you can do to change that behaviour because if you do try, you are partaking in the illusion of taking control of the situation.

b. *The push into irrelevance*

Stemming from the illusion of control is the need to be more and more relevant. Age is not on the mother-in-law's side and neither is her health. Her body isn't what it used to be. And then there is always another sore reminder of a lost youth – her uterus that has gone out of business. It was her well of life, youth and vitality but now lies as a rudimentary organ in her body. Nature has told her she will not bear a child anymore.

Menopause is the biggest push into irrelevance that a woman can receive (if she so wishes to perceive it that way). In fact, feeling irrelevant in the scheme of things due to menopause is another manifestation of embedded misogyny. A woman is supposed to bear fruits and be useful. And our granny generation was that once upon a time. Highly resourceful, highly dependable. The machinery of baby-making and baby-rearing is in the hands of the next generation and that is a bitter pill to swallow. It is a power struggle that takes its roots from the subconscious.

c. *The impatience*

Many a mother-in-law has little patience to watch her daughter-in-law figure out how to change a diaper in a swish smooth effort without having poo all over the place. She has zero respect for something called the learning curve. She expects perfection in the first attempt (but trust me when I say this, if her daughter-in-law is perfect at something in the first attempt, then they get competitive. So, it's really a no-win situation). This is the brand of mothers who raised the IIT engineers and doctors by pushing them into more coaching, more studies and more burning-the-midnight-oil. Imperfection and practice are for losers. And because she was busy raising one-dimensional nerd, she had to do everything around the house. The lazy father was the flag bearer of entitlement from patriarchy and seldom helped around. And the children were busy polishing skills they would never really need in real life. The then mother was the sole operator of the household. And if she had to get anything done right, she had to do it herself.

And so, many years later, she screams on the inside when she sees a new mom learn on the job or tread the learning curve or even ask for help from her husband.

d. *The inheritance of hate*

Why do matriarchs behave the way they do with their daughters-in-law? Not with their other relatives, not with their kids and definitely not that way with their sons-in-law. It is because of years of conditioning that a daughter-in-law is a burden. A squatter son-in-law (a *ghar jamaai*) who is leaching resources and not contributing to the household in any way would have been considered as an asset. Whereas, a financially independent daughter-in-law caring for her family, as well as excelling at work, could be viewed as a liability just because she gets her eyebrows done at the parlour every month. The present-day matriarchs learned from their matriarchs who in turn learned from theirs that daughters-in-law are a financial burden. Matriarchs have had poor role models to learn from, how to behave with their subordinates and get away with saying anything and everything to the one below them in the family hierarchy. Years of listening to her own matriarch and suppressing simmering contempt finally finds its release as she passes on inherited scorn and sarcasm to her own daughter-in-law.

e. *The independence that comes with age*

Another factor that comes into play is how we as daughters-in-law are a part of the society where we have much to gain from the society. We have little kids and we need the mother-in-law to babysit the kid for even a simple thing such as going for a bath. We need to be a useful part of the machinery of the family and function in mutual dependency. A woman needs to make it work with her sister-in-law, her mother-in-law and all of the extended family in order to fit in and have her kids accepted as a part of the family. A matriarch used to be in those shoes once upon a time. She has only now outgrown being dependent and can finally speak her mind. Menopause undoes all the need to be intertwined with the fabric of the society. Her kids have grown, she doesn't need to do duty calls anymore and can get away with leaving the household unattended. The need for perfection is less as her days of impressing her mate are also done with (at least in her mind). She can do whatever she pleases and get away with it.

f. *The biased victim*

Psychologists can go tripping over the behavioural analysis of a menopausal grandmother but before we blame everything on her subconscious, we need to stop in the service lane of introspection. Just because she said something rudely or you are sick of her nags, does not make her wrong all the time. At times, even the pearls of wisdom from a mother-in-law will be disregarded just because it came from her mouth. No person is always right or always wrong. And new moms need to be a little more open-minded to age-old wisdom. Do not reject their knowledge just because they are perhaps less educated than you. They have grown in a different time with fewer opportunities that you and I have been taking for granted for years. Their education might be less but their years of experience, the wisdom gathered from raising their own kids and their best intentions should not be discounted as not valuable. It is really hard to look at the positives when you just want to bang the door shut and block all of her gyaan out of your room.

My advice – Sleep on it. Next morning filter out the real advice from the nagging and you will hopefully find gold. Take everything with a pinch of salt. And even then, if you feel she is in the wrong, come read this section to know you are not alone.

Saboteur #3: The generation that was raised on formula

Rebecca was taken care of by her mother at her *maika* (maiden home) after her delivery but one pitfall Rebecca wasn't aware of was that her mother was a lurking brand ambassador of formula. Every day she would bicker under her breath how the baby wasn't fed enough and how it is important for every mother to give the bottle to the baby. She said bizarre things like, 'Look how thin your milk is compared to formula! The baby isn't getting enough food!' Just because her little baby was particularly clingy to the mother in the evenings, the grandmother would take that opportunity to preach the importance of formula. When Rebecca would argue back, the mother would resign and then bring out her big guns.

'All of you were fed formula and you grew up to be so healthy, but I am wrong, *na*. Yes, my kids are going to teach me how to raise children now.' This tug of war between the mother and daughter was a daily affair and quite exhausting for Rebecca. Even though she was planning on staying for three months with her mother, she asked her husband to pick her up once she completed six weeks on the pretext of missing him, to save her baby from Nani's formula.

Analysis

The mother was no doubt an angel, albeit a misguided one. A lot of present-day grandmothers are flag-bearers of the formula. The current granny generation was the young mother generation two or three decades ago. And their baby-raising days coincide with the peak of formula publicity.

In the first half of the 1900s formula came into the lives of the mothers in the West. With campaigns mounted by formula manufacturers (obviously), this wonder food was the new thing every baby needed. It was tailor-made for the baby according to the advertisements. Suddenly everyone was running short of breastmilk. We were not mammals who could feed their young ones anymore. We were consumers who consumed more food out of packages and told our newborns to do the same. Women were joining the workforce in hordes; they were on television and were progressing in leaps and bounds. Maternity benefits and leaves were not yet a part of the discussion in the male-dominated-work-environment and formula was the saviour for the careers of the modern women. Soon the wave of formula swept into India along with feminism and globalization, bringing foreign food and culture into our lives.

The mother of Caucasian build (the Americans and Europeans) gave birth to bigger babies than the humble build of Asian mothers could. Our babies were tinier, and might I add, darker complexioned than the blue-eyed cherubs of the West. The television was a window into the lives of the Westerners. And Indians wanted that rosy, blue-eyed cherub, too. There was a common myth floating around that the Western baby is chubbier because he gets the richer formula feeds whereas the Indian baby is breastfed like one gareeb (the poor). And the Indian man, woman and child is programmed to want to be like the westerners (we still try to copy their accents, their quinoa and their formula feeding). And thus, formula was propagated as the best food for the baby.

On the other hand, doctors were brainwashed by extensive campaigns from manufacturers into prescribing their 'new and improved' formula to young impressionable mothers as the best for their baby. And when an 'expert' (read: the doctor) says the baby is lagging in growth, needs more feeds and that the mother's milk isn't enough, she will believe that, and she will do the best for her baby.

Another confounding factor here is the smart move by the formula manufacturing companies. They did widespread studies and plotted growth charts (for tracking a child's height and weight gain) based on the data of babies who were fed formula. Now I may seem to contradict myself because earlier in the chapter I had equated breastfeeding with growth, but those formula-fed babies were, in fact, piling on more unhealthy weight than their breastfed counterparts. Add to it the practice of feeding by the clock rather than on demand and you have a recipe for childhood obesity. When a baby is fed on demand and on the breast, his hunger and appetite are respected. Formula was just responsible for appetites that babies had little control over. The mothers of the last generation were in fact raising future obese individuals. The childhood chubbiness is now adult diabetes, heart disease and an expanded waistline.

Rebecca's mother was from the generation that predominantly gave formula to their babies. And she is not to blame. Blame the formula producers and the army of doctors they misled. Her mother was just hardwired into believing that formula was needed by every baby. She was just doing what she thought was best for her grandkid.

Saboteur #4: Victim Blaming

Lactation comes with more than its share of difficulties. There are a lot of technical issues to manoeuvre through, physical hurdles and emotional ones too. Many matriarchs have the tendency to rubbish the issues new moms have just because they didn't have them. If the granny did not know what mastitis was, then the new mother does not have the problem. The issue at hand, rather than getting prompt medical attention, is just brushed off and willed to go away by denial. Who wants to spend time, money and resources on a daughter-in-law anyway?

One patient was struggling with retracted nipples. She was having a hard time getting the baby to latch and the nurses did their best to help her. Instead of being supportive and encouraging of the struggling new mother, the mother-in-law would say, *Ye toh aadhi aurat hai* (she is an incomplete woman).

One patient who was struggling with mastitis (breast inflammation) and had a high fever and breast pain was told by her own mother, *neeyat honi chahiye doodh pilane ki. Isliye ye sab ho raha hai* (You should have the intention to feed your child. Then you wouldn't have such problems.)

A newborn baby was openly persecuted and shunned by her own Dadi. It was because her birth was preceded a few days by the death of her son-in-law. As expected, the new mother and her newborn had to bear the blame for it and was only allowed back into the house because her husband had the brains and guts to oppose the gross injustice.

This kind of hate and victim blaming is very rampant in Indian households. Anything that goes wrong in the house – a caesarean, an illness, a death or even something as common as a breast abscess – is blamed on the woman. It is so routinal that I often see victims blaming themselves for falling sick! And you know what. They are right.

A woman's body is so much under the control of her psyche, that by believing that she is responsible for everything wrong that happens in her sphere, she ends up bringing illness upon herself. I know a woman who had spotting and bleeding every time she would have a fight with her mother. Another mother who was doing just fine with breastfeeding her baby, had to resort to milk bottles because she seemed to not make enough milk overnight. What was the cause? Her visiting co-sister, who was rather busty, passed a mean comment on her small-sized breasts. She internalized the shaming she was subjected to and her body began to believe in this lack of belief.

You can move mountains if you believe but when you are blamed for developing nipple cracks and when every second person coming to see you, comments on how you don't seem to be cut out for motherhood, you end up believing them even when you don't want to. And pretty soon your body catches up. Your fatigued brain and exhausted body have lower physical and emotional immunity. A new mother deserves the protection, care and support at par with what the baby deserves. The more support and belief a mother finds from those around her, the more likely she is to succeed in breastfeeding. We are not just cells and tissues. The consequences of our body's health on our psychological well-being is more far-reaching than imagined.

Even doting husbands, loving nanis, caring friends and concerned neighbours have a hand in victim blaming. If she isn't able to feed her baby for whatever reason, her intentions are questioned. One husband just shrugged his wife off and told her to start formula when she complained about her breastfeeding troubles. We expect the world from the new mother but as a society, we are less than willing to put in the investment required by us for the mother and child. If a woman gets support and care from the bureaucrat in the parliament to the know-it-all masseuse who comes to massage her baby, she is more likely to succeed in feeding her baby and sustaining it. The bureaucrat is the one who will implement laws in the healthcare system that are more conducive to feeding in public and have more relaxed and accommodating maternity benefits. And as for the highly-opinionated masseuse? She knows just how to get under our skin, doesn't she? One snide comment from the maid or maalishwali can leave our fatigued brain spiralling into self-doubt for the rest of the day.

It is easy for a doctor to advise the patient to 'not take stress'. Well, we don't always take it and there are enough people handing out stress to us. 'Lifestyle modification' and 'stress control' are just loose lazy prescriptions in medical practice and more often a footnote. Active counselling and more approachable healthcare providers are the need of the day rather than busy doctors throwing a pill at the problem. This brings me to the role of healthcare providers and their shortcomings in being supportive of breastfeeding.

The Healthcare Providers

Now, let us look at how our Healthcare providers disappoint us at times.

Saboteur #1: Sticky negativity

When Shantamma had just delivered her little girl, she was often overwhelmed while breastfeeding her baby. She breastfed, starting on the right, went to the left side and had to at times feed her on the right again. She was tired, but she was happy. That was until her mother arrived. She and her husband had known the inevitability of Shantamma and her mother locking horns after the baby's birth and were mentally prepared. On the day of discharge, when the grandmother complained to the doctor about Shantamma's inadequate milk (because the baby would suck for long), the doctor examined her latch and positioning and approved of both but instead of assuring them to be patient, the doctor rather carelessly started the new mother on Perinorm tablets (a milk production booster).

Shantamma later tells me how her determination to breastfeed came a little undone when she heard her doctor say that she might be making less milk. What the doctor did was detrimental to Shantamma's budding self-confidence as a new mother. As she continued to breastfeed and mentally block out her own mom at home, Shantamma found it harder to cope. On her follow-up visit with her doctor, she mentioned how she barely slept and how the baby was sucking non-stop. The doctor smiled politely and asked her to try a pacifier.

Sucking continues being the one-stop solution to all of baby's problems. And the baby is not the only one who benefits from this non-stop suck-fest. The mother's milk production gears up to meet the increasing demands of the growing baby but that does not mean the mother lose her mind by having the baby attached to her for twenty-four hours a day. Once in a while, rocking and singing him to sleep, or just handing over the baby to the father and running off to nap is also important for the mother's survival! Many advocates of exclusive breastfeeding have found themselves ignorant of the concept of baby sucking for comfort. And they have introduced pacifiers to the baby to fulfil the need for sucking for comfort. Giving a pacifier to the baby, especially in the first month, is like throwing a spanner at the spokes of milk production. The breast is deprived of its stimulation (which comes from sucking only) and the pacifier is not going to yield any gold by being sucked upon.

The baby's sucking needs are met by the pacifier, but the breasts' sucking needs are not met *because* of the pacifier. The first one month is hard but you have to take one hour at a time, take power naps and brave your way through the haze of sucking marathons. A pacifier will not benefit you if you want to exclusively breastfeed.

Analysis

Shantamma was already getting a lot of negativity from her mother. In addition, her doctor did not know much about the basics of breastfeeding. On the third day after birth, she carelessly prescribed a drug for the patient's 'less production' superimposing on all the doubt that floated around the patient. Slowly, yet surely, Shantamma internalized from her doctor as well as mother that she may not be cut out to exclusively breastfeed. On her follow up, an actual physical saboteur – the pacifier, was thrown into the picture. The more the baby used the pacifier, the less the breast got stimulated to up its milk production. Eventually, on the third week weight measurement, the couple discovered their baby's weight gain was not as expected. The pacifier was the actual culprit – her child's sucking needs were not met by real nutrition but, rather, a dummy nipple. The paediatrician asked them to start two additional formula feeds a day. This in turn became alternate breast and bottle feed over time. And by the end of the six weeks, Shantamma's attempts at breastfeeding were thwarted successfully by a BPA-free bottle and an orthodontic pacifier.

Women tend to pick out the negative and hold on to it way more ardently. It's way easier to not believe. The doctor had sowed the seed of doubt in her heart. In addition to not encouraging, the doctor told the mother to unlatch the baby in fifteen minutes. Smaller babies are slower suckers. On an average, a baby of less than a month old will suck for a total of forty minutes on both sides. It could be for as short as twenty minutes or go on for as long as one hour. They nap in the middle very often and a drowsy sucking session is a rather slow one. Her doctor should have told her to try to alternate methods of pacifying, should have explained the need for sucking for comfort, advised the grandmother to be supportive and should have reassured them both about the new mother's abilities.

Saboteur #2: Flagrant acts of sabotage

Swapna delivered her baby with a lot of difficulty. The baby's head wouldn't descend, and the doctor had to use vacuum pump for the delivery. Due to respiratory distress during delivery, her baby was kept back in the hospital for observation while Swapna was sent home. The new mother was not even allowed to see her child for the first seventy-two hours. Her milk lay ignored in her breast, the baby got a skin to glove contact with a doctor rather than the skin to skin with his mother and the mother's colostrum was just wasted while the baby was given bottle after bottle of formula.

From what I have seen, this kind of separation of mother and child happens very often in the middle east. The distance between the baby and mother after birth had set up a series of events which resulted in irreparable sabotage of their breastfeeding relationship. Swapna pumped her milk to keep it flowing right from Day 1 but sadly, her baby who was never given any exposure to her breast, wasn't able to latch onto her breast after being discharged from the hospital. In his tiny life, his mouth was used to the elongated shape of the artificial teat rather than the mouthful of his mother's breast. A baby is very sensitive to the oral stimulation he receives in the first few days of his life. He will develop a strong preference towards holding his tongue in a certain way to feed on the basis of his first few experiences.

There was no lactation expert available to help the mother re-establish her breastfeeding. I advised her to start feeding the baby her pumped milk with a small spoon from a cup to make him unlearn the bottle latch, but many tiny babies resist such feeding with all their might. He was used to milk coming gushing into his mouth from the bottle, so he had no patience for this paced method of feeding. Swapna couldn't last a day with this method. So, she took a step back and continued to pump and feed the baby by a bottle with a few formula feeds interspersed in between. Swapna was motivated and educated. Yet, she could not succeed due to the irreversible damage her doctors had done to her breastfeeding by the unnecessary separation. The mother and baby should not be separated after birth. The mother should have been admitted for the baby's sake. In fact, if the baby was in respiratory distress, he should have been placed between the mother's breasts for regulation of his respiration and temperature. It is way more effective than placing the baby in an ICU or incubator.

Saboteur #3: Doctors who are under-educated or over-certified business people

I write this section with a heavy heart and an apologetic hand. I have been a patient, a doctor and a listening ear in my life. I have witnessed amazing practitioners succumb to the pressure of time and prescribe more and counsel less. Brilliant minds of experienced doctors have been bedazzled by big pharma and their blatantly untruthful claims. Doctors have been drugged by the addiction of the power that comes with the promise of a new wonder drug and patients have been burnt in the ashtray of their side-effects. Honest physicians who slog to not over-prescribe and try to counsel more are left wanting for time and money for their honest, hard work. I have had the honour and privilege to work in a hospital with some of the most brilliant minds who first questioned everyone high up in the hierarchy of the medical system, rejected more drugs and prescribed more compassion.

Being a doctor comes with a great duty to ensure that every patient and every person you interact with stands to benefit from you. Loosely throwing medical jargon at the patient, discouraging breastfeeding and encouraging formula feeding as a shortcut to ensuring weight gain for the baby are just criminal in my opinion. We, as doctors, have been given very little education in nutritional sciences and lactation. The practical concepts that play a role in milk production are just not imparted in the curriculum. The extent of personal history we are taught to take is this one line: 'Do you smoke or drink?' Well, a woman who has just delivered isn't doing any of those, I am quite sure, but nobody is asking her the question: 'Who was sitting and bugging you the last time you tried to breastfeed?' These questions will solve more problems and increase the rate of breastfeeding than ridiculous drug prescriptions and formula feeding suggestions.

Lactation is a grey area between the gynaecology and paediatric department. Dedicated lactation consultants are few in our country and fewer are experts in the field. Not many doctors are aware of a trustworthy lactation specialist they routinely could send their patients to. The lactation issues are just swept under the carpet and a brand of formula is often forced into the lives of the parents.

Another glaring flaw in the healthcare system is the treatment of a new mother as a single person rather than deeply connected to her entire family as a unit. Routine lactation service lacks a holistic history-taking of the woman's emotional health and social well-being. This aspect of the mother's life needs to be given as much significance as the technical issues. The stressors in the woman's life such as lack of support or too much of support (read: interference) are barely given their due. Lactation assistance needs to be more proactive. New mothers need to be inspected at their homes for follow up and breastfeeding aid, rather than be made to wait in lines at an OPD for healthcare that is barely there.

A stronger network of lactation specialists, perhaps experienced nurses, nutritionists, general practitioners and family physicians trained in this discipline would be a better choice for lactation care rather than paediatricians and obstetricians. I do not wish to malign this noble profession. The system is flawed. The doctors are already overburdened with a burgeoning patient load and a footfall target to meet. It is nice to fantasize about the doctor who will devote time, empathize and be patient with you. Perhaps a doctor-cum-counsellor-cum-lactation expert rolled into one but even the noblest ones have their hands tied down by a dearth of professionals and the trappings of a healthcare system that is all in favour of health and less so of care.

Bumps in breastfeeding

1. Mastitis

Mastitis is the inflammation of the breast. It could be the beginning of an infection and is often reversible at this stage. The breast has redness, is warm to the touch and you could feel feverish. As time passes breast pain could start.

First Aid for mastitis:

a. Tepid sponging with wet wash cloth as required. Adjust the water temperature to your comfort level.

b. Reduce breast pain and pain of sore nipples with paracetamol or a paracetamol/ibuprofen combination. There is no point suffering and worsening your condition.
c. Continue breastfeeding. Don't stop breastfeeding just because your breasts do not look or feel okay. In fact, the principle of treating mastitis taught at the La Leche league (a breastfeeding support group) is 'Empty breasts, lots of rest'.
d. Get help from your partner if it's just the two of you. Ask him to take leave and help out with taking care of the baby, fixing the meals and letting you sleep. If the mastitis will progress to a breast abscess, he will have hell to pay then. So, it's better he lets you rest for a day or two rather than take a prolonged emergency leave later.
e. Breast exercise: Bend forward and hold your breasts. Jiggle your breasts by supporting them gently with your cupped hands. This exercise improves blood flow and lymphatic drainage and prevents from progression of the breast inflammation to a breast infection.
f. When to see your doctor: If you can feel a clogged milk duct (a lump), have a spiking fever lasting more than forty-eight hours or if you see your skin thinning over the breast, it is better to get your doctor's opinion. A clogged milk duct or a breast abscess could be forming within. This will require initiation of antibiotics or drainage of the abscess.

After the birth of my second child I had a lump in my breast accompanied by fever. Like an idiot I sat and squeezed at the lump to remove the milk trapped in it and ended worsening it. My simple mastitis turned into a breast abscess and my doctor had to cut open my breast and drain the pus. It sounds scary, looks scary and feels like a one-way trip to hell but if you are a mother who couldn't succeed at breastfeeding her firstborn, you can tolerate anything and continue to breastfeed your second child despite a breast abscess. I did not miss even one feed because my doctor reassured me that pus in the body will find its way out and drain through the skin and not through the nipple. My doctor gave me a thumbs up to feed from the affected breast and I did. It was really as simple as that.

2. Nipple cracks, soreness

Cracked nipples were one of the worst calamities that struck me personally. I had the evilest nipple cracks with half the nipple tissue gnawed away by my son's toothless latch. There was a time I thought my nipple was going to fall off. In my case I had received too much of conflicting free advice from everyone around me. The negativity from some doctors and a lack of belief by those around me in my ability to breastfeed, all compounded my problem and caused me to stress at every breastfeeding session.

Nipples are delicate and have to toughen up to the prolonged latch and suck of the baby. The pressure from the gums wears out the nipple tissue and causes circular shaped cracks which look more obvious when the nipple is erect. I am not delving into the nitty gritty of latches and baby holding positions because it is best for you that experienced personnel such as a nurse or a lactation expert look at what you are doing with the baby. Breastfeeding is rather instinctive. Yet if you feel you need ideas, refer to the scores of information online about different holds and positions. The rule of thumb is, 'If it feels right, then it probably is right. If it doesn't, then get someone to look at it.'

The three nipple creams I recommend are mother's own milk, honey and ghee. These are some items you have already fed your baby probably in the form of the pre-lacteal feed I had mentioned. Apply honey on your nipple before each feed in the first one week or more of the baby's life. The baby will lick at the honey and that gentle lick will relax your nipples and extend them. Once the muscles of your nipples relax, the nipples will get erect and the baby wouldn't have to tug at it to get milk. The instant glucose provided by the honey will pacify the baby and make his latch gentler.

If you are scared and stressed at the beginning of each feed, the nipple muscles tense up and the baby yanks at it to get a good mouthful thereby hurting the nipple. After each feed, express a bit of breastmilk, apply on the nipple and let it air dry. The antibodies in the milk will protect the nipple. If you feel your breast is sticky because of the honey or milk, then wash gently with water. Apply soap on your breasts only once a day during bath time. You can apply ghee between feeds if your nipple is getting dry or sore. The oil you use for cooking is also fine as a moisturizer. Also, do not go obsessing over the source or brand of honey and ghee. Make sure you give the baby the same thing you eat. Your milk will protect the baby against the bacterial spores or contaminants present.

3. Fungal infection

This can occur any time while breastfeeding and often the mother and child end up passing it back and forth. If you feel a searing or a sharp pain in your nipples throughout the breastfeeding, then do pay a visit to your doctor to rule out a fungal infection. The baby has a curdy looking white patch on his tongue and insides of his cheek. These patches are difficult to differentiate from the normal milk residue on the baby's tongue. So be sure to get your paediatrician to examine the baby's mouth. The doctor will prescribe a mouth paint which you need to apply inside the baby's mouth and on the nipple and some pain medication for the nipple pain.

4. Engorgement

Engorged breasts are painful and ballooned out due to overloading of milk and fluids. It is especially common in the first few days after delivery due to the IV fluids you will be receiving during your time in the labour theatre. The baby finds it hard to latch onto an engorged breast as the nipples flatten out and are difficult to grasp. Almost every mother goes through some degree of engorgement and it is usually a temporary nuisance. Some ways to handle engorgement:

- Make sure you are not overloaded with IV fluids. Often the doctor is out of sight after delivery and the nurses follow the doctor's instructions to the letter without much thought. If you have been receiving IV fluids for more than two hours after delivery and aren't a patient of postpartum haemorrhage, then just press your fingertip into the skin around your ankle. If the skin presses and stays in for a few seconds (something like kneaded dough) then you are probably overloaded with fluids. Request the nursing staff to look into the problem.
- If your breasts are already engorged, then draining them by breastfeeding is often a quick way to get some relief. You can express some milk in the bathroom to make your breasts soft or just press the base of your nipple with your fingertips till the nipple area gets soft enough for the baby to latch on to. The baby will do the rest of the job.
- Help in draining breast fluids by moving them around gently to facilitate lymphatic flow.
- If your breasts are red because of engorgement use an ice pack to relieve the inflammation.

5. Low milk supply

If you feel your milk supply is indeed low, then seek the help of your local lactation consultant at the earliest. Often reassurance is all that the mother needs. If that isn't possible, remember the simple mantra 'demand meets supply'. Pump between feeds to get your milk flowing.

Methi seeds are excellent promoters of milk production. Make sure you have a stock of methi laddoos before you deliver. Also, herbal supplements such as Lactare tablets are a natural way to boost your milk production. Some of my patients take Lactare every ten days or so (for a period of two–three days) to boost their milk supply as the baby's appetite revs up. Your doctor can also prescribe a metoclopramide tablet if there is an actual low milk supply.

6. Flat/inverted nipples

Nipples come in all shapes and sizes. Keep a look out for the shape of your nipple during pregnancy. If you feel they are flat, then start drawing them out with your index finger and thumb three–four times a day. If your normal nipples look flat after delivery, they are more often due to engorgement. Such nipples are deemed flat by an inexperienced intern if he/she comes for your post-delivery check-up. Work closely with a lactation expert/OB-GYN if you have nipple trouble. Pumping with a breast pump is an effective way to help draw nipples out.

7. Is your baby a cluster feeder?

Most people say their babies feed every two–three hours. However, on some days, you will find your baby will be a sucker round the clock and for a good six–eight hours and naturally you will be on 'cow duty' – udderly fantastic? I think not! You will be frustrated and have lots of doubt whether your milk is enough for the baby and might even contemplate reaching out for a bottle. Please don't! Welcome to the world of cluster feeders. Babies have days when they feed every hour for eight hours straight. Much like we binge-watch a popular TV show on occasion. When the baby has to eat, he has to eat. This could be to increase the milk supply by providing the suck stimulus, it could be a growth spurt, an appetite spurt or just filling up on resources for a big night in. A cluster feeder can drive a mother nuts but if you are prepared for it mentally, then you can perhaps even enjoy it!

My second born was a cluster feeder when she turned two weeks old. She would begin her milk fest at 12 a.m. and go on till sunrise! She would suck every hour and that feed session itself would be close to an hour. So, she was pretty much going back and forth between both breasts. Babies suck for food, babies suck for comfort but this one blurred the lines between both. It is a nightmare to have a cluster feeder. You get dehydrated and ravenous. Be sure to have someone to help you out if your baby is a cluster feeder. Keep a bottle of water close by to hydrate yourself often. Keep snacks within arm's reach on your nightstand. Have a source of entertainment at hand to look forward to. Update your friends on your adventures with your newborn. If you plan ahead for a cluster feeding session, then it will be less of a burden. But limit your screen time or reading time to not more than half an hour to one hour. You need rest.

One thing most mothers compromise on during such sessions is rest for the back. You have had nine months of carrying a baby inside of you. After that if you spend more than half your day sitting, your already exhausted and weakened back muscles will not forgive you. I am going to come out and say it. Feed the baby lying down. Grandmoms are taking up arms across the world but I will take a bullet for this cause! (Most grannies don't allow the newborn to be fed lying down because they fear the breast might suffocate the baby.) Just like you should get some shut eye even if you cannot fall asleep, similarly let your back rest even if you are awake. Being a new mom is hard and the best rest you can probably get is assembling the broken pieces of power naps and being horizontal in the name of getting sleep.

Lying down and feeding is the best thing you can teach yourself as a new mother. It might be scary at first (will I suffocate my baby?) and difficult to find the best position you can shove your boob in the baby's mouth and feel rested too, but it will all be worth it. You can feed as small as a newborn baby lying down. As long as the baby is over 2.75 kgs and your consciousness levels are not compromised by any drugs, you should be able to do it.

Formula for Success

I am not one to bite the hand that feeds her son. I fully support breastfeeding but don't wish to put formula manufacturers out of business. Not everything is under one's control, and shit happens. I was determined to breastfeed but got overwhelmed with too much free advice and too little guidance. I desperately clung to breastfeeding to the point of driving myself crazy. Ultimately, it was formula milk that saved my crumbling world and my son's halted weight gain.

Then again, there are two sides of the story. I still do have a problem with the way formula has been marketed through history. Public health campaigns have traditionally described the 'benefits of breastfeeding', comparing health outcomes among breastfed infants against a reference group of formula-fed infants. This approach implies that formula feeding is the norm while breastfeeding is a plus. The campaigns for formula have glorified breastmilk and, in its afterglow, is the formula standing just in second place. That is hardly the truth. Breast milk is not a new and improved version of formula but the plain old normal. Breast milk is what every baby should get.

The bonus of going au naturel

Another reason to embrace the breast would be the cost factor nobody has told you about.

One ounce is equal to 30 ml fluid roughly. Formula is prepared by using one ounce of water for every scoop of formula powder. So instead of working with ml I am going for ounce. Please note: different formula brands have different mixing ratios and this is the most common ratio I have seen in India, so I am working with one scoop per ounce.

Number of ounces of milk required a day in the **first month** – 3 ounces a feed, every 3 hours = 8 feeds a day x 3 ounces = 24 ounces a day.

6–8 ounces per feed every 4 hours from **2–6 months** = 25–30 ounces a day.

Number of ounces consumed = 4680 ounces over 6 months.

Each ounce of milk requires one scoop of formula which is 4.6 grams

87 scoops of formula in 400 g box of formula

54 boxes of formula (each costs around ₹300) required over the first 6 months.

300 rupees x 54 boxes over 6 months = ₹16,200

Over the next six months, the baby is going to be taking solids and be drinking varying amounts of formula. I am just going to do one big lazy round off of the baby needing half the amount of formula for the next six months.

So, about ₹8,000 spent on formula for the next six months.

Total money spent on formula in the first year = ₹16,200 + ₹8,000 = ₹24,200.

A good brand of feeding bottle costs ₹450.

And you need to have a minimum of two bottles at a time for the baby.

Say each bottle lasts three months and you replace nipples monthly. A two-piece pack of nipples cost = ₹350.

Bottle cost for 6 months = (4 bottles x 450 per bottle) + (4 months x 350 per 2-piece nipple pack) = ₹3,200.

Total money spent on feeding equipment = ₹3,200 x 2 = ₹6,400.

Cost of gas to boil water to sterilize bottles – ?

Cost of water – ?

I am not even doing this calculation. You will argue that a breastfeeding mother needs to drink more water and eat more food so let me balance out the cost of fuel and water against this point. Okay?

Cost of pacifier = ₹200. Need approximately one pacifier every month and a half.

Number of pacifiers needed in first year – 8.

Total cost of pacifiers = 8 x 200 = ₹1,600.

Cost of other accessories – bottle covers (₹250 for pack of two) – assuming you need about 6 bottle covers in one year – 250 x 3 = ₹750. Cost of thermos – ₹500.

Cost of nipple/bottle cleaner = ₹230.

Cost of baby bottle detergent 1 litre pack = ₹450.

Assuming that one litre pack lasts a month – 450 x 12 months = ₹5,400.

Cost of sterilizer: Some mothers buy this for travel or home use. The best-selling option on Amazon costs ₹3,500 after discount but I am not even going to add this as many Indian moms use the plain old boiling water for sterilizing the bottles.

Also, formula is so often wasted. But I will not take that into account, too.

A formula doesn't cost just in terms of food bought from the store versus what nature provides. It also costs the baby in terms of health, both short-term and long-term. Formula fed babies fall sick more often and also for longer durations but again, every child is different. So, I am adding only two extra episodes of illness for a formula-fed child in the first one year of his life.

Cost of paediatrician consultation = ₹500

Cost of medicines = ₹500

Total cost for 2 visits = (500+500) x 2 = ₹2,000

I am not being weird by adding this cost. I just want to highlight the importance of the immunity advantage offered by breastmilk. Hence, I felt I had to acknowledge this cost too.

A breastfeeding mother does not get her periods for the first six months minimum and it could be a period-free streak for up to a year for some lucky mothers. A mother feeding the baby formula gets her periods super early in about three–four months post-delivery.

I spend about ₹200 on each cycle and I have heavy flow periods lasting six days.

Cost of pads because of early periods (8-month period free advantage for a breastfeeding mother) –

₹200 x about 8 months of excess periods = ₹1,600.

Total cost:

You save about ₹42,450 in the first year by breastfeeding your baby.

You are welcome.

6

BODY IMAGE ISSUES

A woman's body is one of her most cherished blessings and what she does with her body is her decision. However, no matter how hard we try, there is no getting away from the fact that our body is never going to be fully ours till we, the women, carry the responsibility of bearing children. We share our body for nine months with the child and what happens to our body in that time is mostly out of our hands.

I may sound anti-motherhood when I say we lose control of our bodies. Don't get me wrong. I love being pregnant and I love being a mother (on most days). I also know that we have some degree of vanity and hate what it does to our bodies. From the run-of-the-mill stretch marks to the mortifying loss of bladder control, mothers have to go through it all. We have to ultimately make our peace with the new 'heavily' altered body, but it takes us time, and, might I add, agony to reach that stage of self-acceptance.

One of my patients, Anaya, was a moderately built thirty-year-old who planned her first child when she was well settled in her career. She had a healthy and uneventful pregnancy apart from the fact that she got very large rather quickly during her pregnancy. She was never really big bottomed and could wear jeans and tights without ever being very conscious. But during her pregnancy, her bottom just packed in the pounds and it began to get embarrassing. Her colleagues often joked that her butt was pregnant, and she would try to just laugh it off but pregnancy hormones had made her extra sensitive to such jokes. During breaks to go out for a stroll and stretch her legs, she would often find herself engaged against her will in discussions focused entirely on her butt lasting over five minutes. By the time the third trimester rolled in, her bottom had grown huge, and she would find herself crying in the ladies' toilet every other day after having received a volley of jokes from her colleagues for her roundness. It was taking a toll on her health and sleep. Despite being in great health, she ended up applying for her maternity leave two months before her due date just to escape the living horror that her workplace had turned into.

While Anaya battled her issues with excess weight, Meenal had developed the issue of varicose veins on her legs which appeared one fine day in her second trimester. In her words, 'When I developed varicose veins during my pregnancy, I was distraught. And my veins were popping and were obvious on my pale skin. I had tiny pink veins flaring out on my ankles. I had those blue-green veins snaking over my legs. I had these bluish eruptions on my shin. The back of my thigh had a grey coloured mosaic-like pattern. It was as if all my veins suddenly decided to put on a show. I stopped wearing shorts for my daily run after a few aunties remarked at how weird my legs looked. I wanted to deal with it like a medical problem that would go away. But people did not let me. My husband often cracked jokes about my legs. I delivered my son four months ago and I still need to mentally get over my fixation with the varicose veins (which haven't gone yet). Because every other night, I still Google images of varicose veins to get some solace in knowing that other people share my condition and insecurity in some part of the world.'

Swati, on the other hand, was fixated with another part of her body – her belly. Her stretch marks were not the silvery kind but instead were of a dark brown colour. She did not realize she was not any different from others (she had assumed that's what tiger stripes meant) till her sister cried out loud on seeing her belly when she once lifted her top to breastfeed the baby. Her sister's shock was shortly relayed to her mother and aunt and all of them fussed about her not being able to wear a saree ever because of these hideous stretch marks. Over time her stretch marks faded away but her low self-esteem stayed on.

Our bodies and minds are willing to adapt to bear our precious children but society's rigid mindset of what we should look like forces us to take two steps back and enter into self-doubt. It is not just the weight gain but also hair loss and skin changes that get rudely picked on and commented upon by people. It is a checkmate of sorts.

Right after marriage, the woman is badgered every month with questions about pregnancy but once she has the baby, the same people want the woman to look like a new bride instead of a new mother.

The Sad Plight of a Woman

One person asked me the following question online:

> I had a caesarean section a month ago. I had gained 25 kg during my pregnancy. If I start my weight loss programme such as fast walking, exercises, diet foods – will it affect me or my baby? What is the right time for both of us to start losing weight? How many months does it take to recover from C-section stitches? Kindly answer these questions. This is very important to me. I hate to see myself so fat.

Before I delve into answering this, I would like to deconstruct it to understand what's going on in this person's mind. This new mother has not even completed her six weeks postpartum and she is eager to shed the weight which she deems unwanted and undesirable. As a mother of two children, I understand her angst very well but the poor woman needs to realize that now is not the time to agonize over beauty. The second part of her question emphasizes the need for quick solutions to her big problem. She wants to quickly go on 'brisk walks' and shed her fat by some miraculous 'diet foods'. After asserting how she is in a tearing hurry to lose all those extra pounds, does she pause to finally ask something relevant to her health? What would be the right time for 'both of us' to lose weight. Dear, do you really want both you and your baby to lose weight? And almost as an afterthought does she ask the most pressing question of all – about her recovery. To compensate for the distracting question about her stitches, she rebounds back to her weight issue.

First of all, dear new mother, step away from your weighing scales. It is not your friend right now. Let me try to help you by breaking down your twenty-five kilograms weight gain. All of it has not gone and has piled on your butt and belly. Your baby must have been 3–3.5 kg out of the twenty-five. Then there is a lot of water retention that occurs during pregnancy. Your baby was bouncing in some of that retained water which is the amniotic fluid. Your blood vessels filled up with more blood and the increased volume was to make sure the blood supply to the placenta and your growing precious child was never compromised. Even when you sweat too much or drank too little, your body made sure the baby was well looked after by this increased circulation. When you sat, stood or rushed to do endless chores, the placenta and the baby were always getting their life fluid. Your breasts retained more volume than your bra is capable of containing. The perked-up mounds your breasts had become were growing to manufacture and store milk for the baby who would soon get nourished from them. They had more tissue, more fat and more blood in them.

As soon as you delivered, the baby, the placenta and the blood escaping from your body brought down your weight by about six to seven kilograms. You achieved instant gratifying weight loss in the delivery room! Love handles, true to their name, are made of love. The excess fat in the rolls of your belly cushioned the child living inside of you. Once the baby is out, the fat nourishes the evacuated home that is now your body. The house needs to be renovated, repainted, patched up and refurnished for your next baby. Or not; but the upkeep has to be done irrespective of your decision to have more children.

Right after delivery, you look at least six months pregnant. That is because, effectively, you kind of are six months pregnant. Your uterus is still very large and filling up a big section of your abdominal cavity. It needs around six weeks to retract, contract and go back to its original tiny size fitting into just the pelvic cavity. Over the next six weeks, you will be losing blood and debris from your uterus in the form of a vaginal flow called lochia. It does not look like period blood, but it is just as annoying. You have to wear sanitary pads and tolerate uncomfortable sensations when you have a sudden flow. This lost blood is more weight loss for you. As for the fat you seem to have so much objection to, it is less than half of the twenty-five kilograms weight that you gained. The six-month pregnant belly will reduce once the uterus has shrunken back. But till then, enjoy the fat-rich foods, laddoos, ghee, milk and jaggery. Your body needs all the protein from the milk, eggs, coconut and *rava* (semolina). The iron from jaggery and dates will make up for all the iron you lose in your postpartum bleeding and pass on in your milk. It needs carbohydrates to fuel your body. Which is like a machine working overtime, trying to recover from delivery and provide nourishment to this tiny person your amazing body has made.

Why We Look the Way We Do After Delivery

Millions of women agonize over their weight and forget to enjoy motherhood. They want the Malaika Arora or the Kareena Kapoor Khan weight loss story. To add to their insecurities are nosy neighbours and relatives who mock them mercilessly. I have had my share of mockery and ridicule. I had just one reply to them, 'If I diet, my baby diets.' That seemed to temporarily shut them up (even though it's not entirely true!). The world is full of people deriving sadistic pleasure from a beautiful woman apparently turning into a shapeless amoeba on producing babies. A man who gains weight by being a couch potato, eating pizza and growing a beer belly is seldom targeted but a healthy woman, who has had a baby a month ago, isn't spared.

The evolutionary reason why such a premium is placed on tiny waists with proportionately wide hips and ample breasts is for attracting a mate. The waist–hip ratio reflects health and fertility in a woman. The breasts signify her ability to feed the offspring that would result from the mating (although in reality breast size does not affect the milk production). The tiny waist has an essential part to play in attracting a mate. It signifies the woman is a virgin, has not had babies and hence it is so tiny. Although virginity and waist size have no real correlation!

In fact, the totally out of whack waist to hip ratio in a new mother is important biologically. If our shape and size are sending signals to our mate, then so is the pear-shaped postpartum body. The big waist is unappealing because it is propagating that it just had a baby and is in no mood to entertain any mating propositions. The body is still reeling from the effects of its last mating and it looks unattractive because it does not want to attract anyone just yet.

This Weight is Not Yours to Lose

The kilo is not the aim. Just because you put on fifteen kilograms does not mean you need to lose fifteen kilos in five months. It may be your body but those kilograms are not yours to dispose of as you please. Those belong to the baby. The fat you put on in your abdomen cannot be burnt off by exercise. This fat was meant to protect your internal organs and the baby during pregnancy and those reserves rightfully belong to the baby. *Research has shown that even seven years post-delivery, mothers who had lost their pregnancy weight had not lost the deeper abdominal fat as opposed to the mothers who breastfed their babies.*[1] The more you breastfeed, the more the deep layers of fat are utilized. There is a saying in Hindi, *Daane daane pe likha hai khaane wale ka naam* (what is allotted cannot be blotted). This stubborn fat that gets stored during pregnancy belongs to the baby and there are no two ways about losing the deeper fat by skipping breastfeeding and hitting the gym.

Losing weight after delivery is very different from regular weight loss.

1. You cannot and should not start right after delivery: The earlier you try to get rid of the weight, the more lethargic and beaten down your body will become. A recovering body needs time and food to heal. Don't strain it by exercise and overthinking about the additional curves you have collected. There will be some amount of weight gain in the first two months after delivery possibly because of your voracious appetite and your prolonged sitting for breastfeeding. And you need to let it be. Also, you must not cut back on your food intake just yet in an attempt to lose weight. Your body needs a good three months to recover.
2. You need to get your muscles back: This is not achieved by strength training but by rest and massage. The postpartum massage is the first step to gaining muscle mass. Sitting or lying in bed for most of the day is the norm after delivery. The massages will help in relaxing your muscles as well as building muscle mass and improving your insulin sensitivity (protects against diabetes).
3. Your hormones need to settle to normal: Give your body time to settle into its pre-pregnancy state. Aside from

the reproductive hormones, oestrogen and progesterone, your other hormones such as growth hormone, insulin, thyroid hormone and cortisol are also off balance. A good nutritious diet (a must) and adequate rest (which will be hard to get) will set the balance right and set you on the path to reclaiming your body.

Nourished and Cherished

When everyone around is being petty and taking joy in ridiculing you for your mom body, please keep calm and eat that extra roti you have been eyeing. The first two–three months after birth you will eat more than a teenage boy having a growth spurt. And it is your right to eat all that food. Starving yourself to lose weight will actually make you pile on more weight and especially in the wrong places such as your belly. Bide your time before you get your revenge body and silence the trolls in your life.

Many husbands sport a cheerful beer belly but have the audacity to tell their wives (who have delivered a baby about four months ago) 'to get her curves back'. It is body shaming at its peak. This woman altered her entire body, bore his child for nine months, risked her life to give birth to that child and her ungrateful husband tells her to get her curves back!

I know we are all very sensitive especially after delivery when our hormones are messing with us. Add to it our sleep deprivation and struggles with post-delivery problems. So, it is only our right to treat our bodies well and keep them well-fed. Your body has gone through so much to give birth to the precious baby. Don't push it into looking sexy just yet.

There is another important reason you should be kind to your body. The more stress you take about your weight, the more your hormones will go into saving mode. Stress from caveman times translated as threat to survival. A stressed body produces more cortisol which is responsible for fat deposition on the belly. Your body and mind need to be on the same team. Train yourself to think of the fat as a temporary guest to help you. You need to give some to get some. *Give your body food and kindness when it really needs it and you will be rewarded with those pounds shed, because your body felt secure and did not see the need to store fat.* One of my friends, a Marwari, was made to drink ghee daily after her delivery. She was fed by a doting mother-in-law and within five months she was back to her pre-pregnancy weight. Had she stressed over her weight and cut down her food intake, she wouldn't have been blessed so soon with the regained vigour and lost weight that we all envy.

Why You Should Lose Weight

On the one hand, there are women in a tearing hurry going down the road to weight loss (with little results) while on the other hand, pregnancy weight is taken as a life-long burden and the woman makes little effort to shed the weight. A need to see quick results and being drawn towards easy fixes is a part of the problem. We all need to understand that this transformation is neither an instant result nor an impossible one. Having patience till a minimum of four to six months before embarking on a workout routine is crucial for allowing the body to change gears.

Most out-of-shape mothers around us seem to fuss more and work less towards their weight goals. It might have been four years since her delivery, but she is still lamenting her fat rolls and not much else. Such moms are seen joining Zumba and salsa classes but are not able to sustain the efforts. *The best time to embark on the weight loss journey is within the first year after childbirth to tap into the advantage offered by your high metabolism after delivery.*

Loss of libido and weight loss

In addition to being fat and undernourished, the modern postpartum woman is also highly unattractive in her own eyes (more than her partner's). Her brain is conditioned to think that she is sexy only at a certain kilo and a certain size and anything over and beyond that is just cringe worthy. If a woman loses her sex appeal in her own eyes, she finds it hard to be attracted to her partner. And the low sexual drive is also, in a way, a self-preservation mechanism whereby the woman does not put herself out for rejection by her partner. The simple logic behind this is that if she isn't available, then she won't be rejected. Her relationship with her partner takes a hit because of these excess pounds which have undermined her self-confidence at a subconscious level.

Exercise and activity not only helps one in losing weight but there are non-reversible changes taking place with even one workout a week. The brain centres which control a woman's mood and personality – the hippocampus and the prefrontal cortex – show growth of brain cells after a half-hour bout of aerobic exercise. The key here is to not adopt the hectic workout routine of the movie star that you have read about. The key is to exercise in such a way that it challenges your body and gets your heart beating. With low stamina after childbirth, even a fifteen-minute stroll around the park could be your workout. It has to start somewhere small and grow from, it rather than somewhere big and fizzle out quite quickly.

Strategies for Weight Loss

Here are some things you can do for a slender body that is sustainable and not a quick-fix, and will help you tone up and feel healthier.

The strategies are:

1. Initial rest and recovery
2. NEAT breaks
3. Eating well
4. Breastfeeding
5. Pacing into a workout routine

The first thing to start you off on your journey to reclaiming your body is taking claim to the rest you deserve. Pregnant and delivery are no simple feats. They drain all of the body's and mind's resources. Recuperation from delivery needs a long time, so go slow on yourselves. Ample rest with few walks around the house and taking care of your own body on extremely broken sleep is a challenge. Some of the things you can do for yourself to make sure your body is well rested:

a. Social media sabbatical: I can't stress on this enough, but these days social media is one of the biggest culprits for women not getting rest after delivery. It is true we are all holed up with a strange crying baby and need to find our old selves, but social media is doing more harm than good to your body.

   The white light from your phones mimics daylight and asks your body to produce less melatonin because the body believes that it isn't night yet. This hormone melatonin is responsible for us feeling fresh during the day and groggy as the night sets in. Going online when your baby is keeping you awake at night messes up with your body clock. In addition, such a messed-up body clock produces less of the satiety hormone leptin. This hormone gives you satisfaction on eating your meal and reduces your appetite. Over many days, as your leptin keeps waning because of night time exposure to light, your appetite is also going out of control and so is your waistline.

b. Mastering breastfeeding lying down: In my chapter on breastfeeding I have highlighted the importance of lying down irrespective of sleep to rest your strained back muscles. Learn to breastfeed lying down early on to ensure you get a better rest.
c. Don't look for a happily ever after: Pregnancy is often viewed as a long wait to the spectacular finish. The only thing is that there is no finish and it isn't spectacular for sure. It is harsh, hard and tough to swallow. Life isn't a movie montage where sleeplessness with a new baby is glorious. Keep your expectations low, don't try to control your day or your baby and take it one hour at a time. Close your eyes even if you aren't able to fall asleep. Shut eye is more rejuvenating for your brain than you would like to give it credit for.

The Science of Weight Loss

When you sit, sleep, talk, laugh, watch TV, Facebook, WhatsApp or Tweet, you are constantly burning fuel and producing heat (that's why dead bodies are cold and alive people warm). There is metabolism at play even during rest – which is your body's machinery constantly at work. In this resting metabolism even if the person is asleep, the breathing, the digestion, repair of cells, fat storage, filtering blood to form urine, the constantly working brain, the muscle tone, all consume energy. This accounts for your RMR or resting metabolic rate. BMR (basal metabolic rate), the term that we so commonly use in gyms to speak about metabolism, and RMR are different from a scientific viewpoint. BMR is used for research purposes and calculated under scientifically produced conditions after an overnight fast. Just to be accurate in my account I will be using the abbreviation RMR.

The Math of Weight Loss

Calories required to be eaten by a man – 2500 calories.

By a woman – 2000 calories.

These calories are required to maintain the current weight of a person weighing 65–70 kg and takes into account energy spent on daily body functions and energy you spend doing your regular chores.

Energy burnt during a half hour jog on an average – 350 calories (depending on the speed and intensity of the jog, the calories spent varies. I am just working with averages to give you an idea).

Energy burnt during the day by RMR – 1500 calories.

Remaining calories – for daily, regular work.

So, basically 70 per cent of your daily calorie intake is consumed for maintenance and upkeep of your body and only about 15–20 per cent of calorie burnt is by working out. Also, we need to take into account lazy days (can't get out of bed), cheat days (the day you skip exercise and binge on dessert), busy days (kid's PTA, dentist appointment), sick days (sniffles), 'first day of period' days and other no-exercise days. Some days you workout extra hard and for extra-long with sincerity. Some people detest workouts, and some thrive because of exercise. Working out regularly and diligently is something I recommend. My patients with less than desired sugar reports and slightly high cholesterol while reeling from the shock of their diagnosis, start off with their exercise routine all pumped up but a month later they run out of fizz. In fact, my own husband is a great example.

Every year my husband sacrifices the money to satiate the demons of the gym. He gets super motivated once a year (maybe his motivation follows the solar calendar?) and decides to do something about his paunch. The first year of our marriage, he decided to get a gym membership for a year because he was getting a great deal (and I am sure his gym trainer was getting a great commission in the bargain). He paid ₹16,000 for that membership. And he went for exactly one day. I kid you not! That was probably the most expensive gym session in human history! In our second year of marriage, he had a kid, had his own start-up and was busy getting his new venture kickstarted. Owing to his busy schedule, he didn't get the gym membership but what he did get were new running shoes and a new pair of swimming trunks. Suffice it to say that I can resell those on eBay and get full price! The third year, he picked a CrossFit gym. It was a pay-per-class kind of membership, so I agreed. And my husband did not let me down. This year again, he went for exactly one class. The recurring gym failure was getting embarrassing for my husband in front of his know-all wife. He did not want to lose face yet again to Mrs I-told-you-so. This time, to impress the gym demon, he found a new way of paying tribute. He made his offering to FitBit. He got it for a great discount (₹6,000 spent). He was rather taken in by his new fixation and was actually doing great. Was. Past tense. The Fitbit now lies ignored in his sock drawer waiting to be charged and used.

Every second person has such a story. They all start with guns blazing but a few days later their motivation is a dying spark. I see women waste money on Zumba one month, purchase a treadmill the next month, a cycle after that and attend five yoga sessions the following month before giving up. Nothing lasts except for that stubborn tummy tyre.

So why am I telling you 'un-success' stories? Because they are unsuccessful. Every person gets motivated for that wedding she has to attend or the old jeans she wants to fit into. Especially new mothers, who are often mocked for their pregnancy weight, are like the drowning person clutching at a straw. They are drowning in body shame and clutching at every exercise class or fad diet coming their way. Life is busy. Kids take up time. There is no time even to unwind in front of some trashy TV show. After becoming a mother, if I get to comb my hair before lunchtime, I am happy. Those first few months post-delivery are nothing short of hectic. Gyms, yoga classes or any other routine don't just take motivation. They take time. And moms don't have much of it! I have been through it all and I empathize. Throwing money at the excess weight isn't going to make it go away. Exercise routine should be regular and sustainable. Rapid weight loss shouldn't be your goal. Sustained weight loss and a body brimming with health and happiness should be.

NEAT indeed

Earlier in this chapter I have mentioned that the standard number of calories a person should consume a day is 2200 calories (it's actually kilocalories but for food speak the word calories is okay). At this point, I would like to introduce you to your new best friend, NEAT. NEAT is short for Non-exercise Activity Thermogenesis. Let's get to know NEAT better (since it's going to be your new best buddy). The word thermogenesis means thermos, which means heat (same root in thermostat and thermometer) and genus which means birth (same root in genetics, genes, genesis). So basically, thermogenesis is heat production. NEAT then, can be simply put as 'heat produced in your body not because of targeted exercise'.

As I had pointed out earlier, RMR comprises 70 per cent of your calories burnt whereas workout uses up a meagre 15 per cent. The remaining 15 per cent goes into your day-to-day activities.

What if we increased that energy spent on RMR and those mundane chores? Some basic math before I dive deeper into my weight loss strategy.

Sitting > Lying down
Standing > Sitting
Walking > Standing
Climbing stairs > Walking

So, if you are talking on the phone rather than lying down or sitting, pace around and talk. If you are lying down checking Facebook and texting, stand up and do it. If you have two floors in your house, rather than telling your household helper to get you stuff from the other floor, climb up and get it yourself. If you have a desk job at an IT firm (like most Bangaloreans do!) which requires you to code for hours on end, take a standing break every hour and stand on your tippy toes for two minutes. And climb two flights of stairs every two hours. Are you addicted to spending money on weight loss programmes just like my husband? Spend that money on an activity tracker and count your steps. Not a big fan of spending money on gadgets? Download an app on your phone and use that to track your activity. Hate these apps and gadgets like I do? Great! Motivate yourself and consciously keep moving and reduce time spent on your bottom!

NEAT basically is increasing your metabolic rate and activity level to lose weight. Focused activity such as exercise is great but of limited value in a super-swamped mother's life for losing weight and keeping it off. Lack of motivation or time or any other reason for an exercise schedule should not stop you from losing weight. Take 'NEAT breaks' to step away from your work and get moving for five minutes.

Watching a movie? Get up and do fifteen squats and two planks (lasting one-minute each) and go back to your movie. This takes just three minutes but what you have effectively done is jump-started your metabolism, got the muscles pumping and risen your blood pressure transiently. Just this much activity will encourage more efficient fat burning for the next few hours.

The mechanism by which NEAT works at burning fat is by stimulating the enzyme hormone sensitive lipase (HSL). This enzyme opposes the fat storing action of insulin and is released when the muscles are active. So, if you stand when you could be sitting, you are increasing the action of this enzyme and promoting the burning of fat in your body. If you do a set of twenty jumping jacks while watching a movie, you boost your heart rate and cause the production of adrenaline by this sudden spurt of activity. The adrenaline released promotes the action of HSL and so do the activated muscles. The sudden aerobic bout boosts your metabolism and prolongs fat burning and post activity oxygen consumption.

Some examples of NEAT breaks:

1. Every time you enter your bedroom, do a plank lasting a minute. Do at least four planks distributed through the day.
2. One set of thirty jumping jacks fifteen minutes before your meal times. Or whenever you find time. Aim for three such sets a day.

3. Do a vigorous dance to a three-minute song twice a day. Just play a song and break into an impromptu routine.
4. Three sets of twenty squats during the day.
5. If you like to jump rope, then you could do one set of fifty.

Now the important thing to take note of here is that these small activity bursts are better at keeping weight off you than doing a rigorous workout and sitting for the rest of the day. Even if you started your day by hitting the gym, the metabolism boost you got by your routine will last only a couple of hours and will slow down as you spend your time sitting through the day. You don't have to do all the exercises I mentioned and try to aim for a few sets. *Don't sit at a stretch for more than two hours.*

Boost Your Metabolism by Eating Well

To take advantage of the big chunk of energy spent in RMR, eat small split meals. When you used to go on a diet you would see your weight shedding rapidly at first to only level off a few weeks later. And the minute you stopped the diet, you would pile it all back on. The body is not here to bend to anybody's whim and fancy. It will be abused and inflamed by all insults thrown at it in the name of crash dieting. But the body is all about self-preservation and protects itself by conserving energy sources when subjected to the torment of wilful starvation that is a crash diet. Hence, it reduces the energy spent on all the processes that go into repair and upkeep of the body which is simply known as your metabolism.

When food is eaten, the metabolic rate of the body increases because of specific dynamic action (SDA). The SDA of the food is the energy spent in digesting and absorbing it. An amount of protein that provides 100 kcal energy takes 30 kcal from the body to digest and assimilate. 100 kcal carbohydrate requires roughly 6 kcal and 100 kcal fat needs 4 kcal to digest. This means that the amount of calories available by these foods decreases by that amount. The energy used for assimilation comes from the food or the body's stores.

The other way by which the metabolism is boosted is that the hormone systems that regulate metabolism (thyroid and adrenals) are activated by eating. More the thyroid hormone in the body, more the metabolism. It is by these simple changes in dietary habits that you can direct your body into a slimming mode.

While SDA of proteins is a great way to eat well and lose weight, be sure to be mindful and practice portion control. Eating unlimited food is going to show up as fat reserves. Too much of protein isn't going to build muscle if you only eat and don't work out. It will get stored as fat.

Eat fermented foods: Include curds (at room temperature) in your diet every day. Try to make idli/dosa batter at least once a week. These promote the growth of the good bacteria in the gut. In a study, subjects were given fermented milk to drink for four weeks on a daily basis. Their belly fat reduced by 8.2 per cent in those 4 weeks. Their body fat percentage and waist to hip ratio also reduced.

Don't swear off oil and ghee: Boiled or raw versions of foods are a pathetic attempt at weight loss. You think you are doing a splendid job at self-control. But fat in food is not equal to fat on butt. This fat dissolves vitamins A, D, E and K and aids in their absorption. It also slows the absorption of glucose from your food and protects you from diabetes.

The first two–three months are the time to eat as you please. Once your body has substantially recovered, your appetite will start to wane off as your body adapts to the demands of breastfeeding. At this point, you can practice moderate portion control to slightly tip your energy balance into negative and start off your weight loss. Continue the five meals a day but your three main meals can be cut down by 25 per cent. For instance, if you ate two rotis at lunch, then bring it down to one and half and you will see results without any mind-numbing or body-stressing hunger.

My personal experience

I lost fourteen kilograms by the time my daughter turned one. I had done exactly one week of yoga at home and one week of cycling. I did go for daily walks when I would take my son out to play with the baby in stroller. His particular knack of running away made me sprint after him daily and that was my unintentional high intensity interval training in a sense! Aside from that, one change in my diet that helped control my portion size was milk. I would have a glass of plain whole milk an hour before lunch and dinner. It would leave me full and satisfied and I would not take that extra helping of rice at my meals.

Many people go for skimmed or semi-skimmed milk to lose weight. As more years have passed and the dairy lobby is still more confused as to which form of milk to support or renounce, evidence has emerged that having whole milk is better for losing weight in the long run. The fat and protein profile of whole milk makes it an excellent food to curb your appetite and prevent you from getting your calories from other inferior sources of carbohydrates. With the rising vegan diet craze, milk and milk products have lost their prime place in our diets as a complete protein. If you don't have lactose intolerance, then be sure to drink up a glass or two in a day.

Pacing into a Workout Routine

You are a different human now. In the process of giving birth to your baby you have also rebirthed as a mother. You may have been physically weaker to start with but now you are more resilient. Don't expect or beat yourself up for not being able to lift weights. The mantra to easing into targeted weight loss is pacing it out. If you start too soon, then your recovering body is abused by this excess stress of activity and you will soon run out of steam. Give yourself a minimum of three months before you start the conventional exercises as well as the NEAT breaks. Before that, take heart in knowing you are not being a slob because of these changes in your lifestyle:

a. Breastfeeding is one of the most important burners of pregnancy fat. You burn a whopping 550 kcal a day by breastfeeding. It is one of the stupidest things when a woman says that she discontinued breastfeeding so that she could head to the gym and lose weight. A half hour jog burns 300 kcal. Here you get to sit on your ass while burning off calories. Isn't that what our dreams are made of?

   Another advantage of breastfeeding is that the fat that is burnt is the deep organ fat which is the dangerous kind that predisposes one to diabetes, heart disease and high blood pressure. Also, the breastfeeding woman in general has a higher metabolism, so more calories are burnt at rest. If you chose to breastfeed for one year, then you get the advantage of a high metabolism for that long.

b. Daily massage for the first forty days will help you gain muscle mass. More muscle mass means a higher metabolism and a faster, more efficient weight loss.

c. A healthy nutritious diet cannot be compromised upon and you need to eat quality nutrition and not run after exotic stuff in search of the holy grail of right food. Stick to your local diets and traditional recipes which will be better accepted and digested by your body. Poor food intake in the name of dieting will predispose you to low energy levels, mood swings and chemical imbalances in the brain which can cause postnatal depression. Protect yourself from hypothyroidism by eating a balanced diet daily. The thyroid hormone will keep up your metabolism.

All women are different and cannot be expected to hit these targets at fixed times, but as a general guideline here is how you can start your exercise routine.

The first two months

a. Keep your activity levels low. Small walks around the house to stretch your legs and a few light ballet like stretches once a day are fine.
b. Make sure you do kegels every day to strengthen your pelvic floor muscles. This will prevent urine leaks when you cough or sneeze or at least mitigate the severity. Every woman gets some degree of urinary incontinence after delivery so take heart in the fact that you are not alone. Tighten your pelvic floor muscles and hold for few seconds. If you can't figure out which muscle to control, then while passing urine try to stop the flow. The muscle which tightens is the one. But kegels are not

supposed to be done while passing urine! At first you will be able to hold the muscle tight for a few seconds but gradually aim for holding for up to ten seconds. After each muscle contraction give a gap of two breaths and do 10 repetitions. Aim to do three such sets in a day.

c. You can start with pelvic floor tilts a month after delivery. Lie flat on your back and stick the small of your back to the surface and repeat ten times. This exercise engages your spine, the muscles and connective tissue around it. The entire trunk and abdominal muscles are strengthened. This is one of the basic steps to core strengthening.

Months three–six

You will feel stronger and more energetic at this stage. Continue with the kegels and pelvic tilts. In addition to those exercises you can:

a. Start going on daily walks six–eight weeks after delivery. A twenty-minute walk in the evening with your baby in the stroller is the ideal workout to begin with. The baby also gets exposed to a different quality of light as opposed to the artificial lighting at home and gets plenty of auditory and visual stimulation out in the open for his little brain's development.
b. Another excellent core workout is swinging on a swing. Just a plain regular playground swing. Harder workouts for your core make you work against gravity and the belly

can sag. Swinging doesn't go against gravity, works easy on your recovering body and is fun! As you swing back and forth, the movements of your legs to keep the swing in motion engage your core and strengthen your abs. It is a gentle exercise and does not tire the core as quickly as other more challenging workouts. The key point I want to remind you here is that your body is weaker than it used to be, so minor challenges in activity levels will be better at strengthening your muscles rather than rigorous workouts you were used to before conceiving. (You might argue that people will judge you or even come up to you and say 'Aunty the swing will break'. Yes, I have been through it too! I think it's time we reclaim our lost childhood joy and bring in swings for adults too!)

Before you begin a workout schedule, get yourself examined by your doctor to rule out diastasis recti. In this condition, due to excess pressure of the growing baby, the abdominal muscles stretch and separate. Lie on your back with your knees bent and feet flat on the floor. Lift your head and neck slightly while feeling for a bulge above and below your belly button. An isolated bulge more than two fingers apart could indicate you have an abdominal muscle separation. Consult a therapist or a doctor for it. Many DIY core exercises do more harm than good, so it is best to get yourself physically examined.

c. Simple *asana*s such as the pelvic bridge, spinal twists, leg lifts, cat pose, tiger pose, can be a part of your at-home yoga routine. I wouldn't recommend you join a yoga class as your day will still be revolving around the baby. The easier you go on yourself in terms of time management, the better it would be on your adherence to a workout schedule. Aim for three yoga sessions a week, each lasting for half an hour. Swinging and yoga were the first exercises I began with about three and half months after my delivery and noticed progress in my tummy tone as well as weight loss. I also learnt to master *chakrasana* (the wheel pose) by practicing it daily. If you already aren't familiar with yoga routines, then you could take a few classes from a yoga teacher to learn the proper form and technique and workout at home daily.

d. To prevent your breasts and belly from sagging, your back should be strong and not excessively curved inwards. Most women face lower back weakness or pain after delivery due to the strain of carrying a baby for nine months. When I had to bend to tie my son's shoelaces after my second delivery, I had to get up like an old grandma clutching my weak back. I was mortified by this disability and started a daily back routine for gaining muscle strength.

   The best back strengthening exercises are (again, get yourself examined for diastasis recti before adopting this workout):

   – The cat stretch and camel hump – This classic yoga pose helps stretch out the back as well as extend it providing flexibility and relief from soreness. Start with this to warm up your abdominals and back muscles. Stand on all fours and raise your neck high while your back dips downwards as you stretch like a cat. Go from the stretching pose to arching your back upwards in the form of a camel hump and hold position for three breaths. Alternate for eight repetitions.

- The lying knee hug – To work on your gluteal muscles (for lower back strength) do the lying knee hug. In this exercise, lie straight on your back and bend your right knee and bring it towards your chest to hug it. While your right knee is drawn to your chest, your left leg will be lifted in the air at a 30° degree angle. Alternate between the legs for eight repetitions.
- Child's pose – Bend your hips and knees with your shins on the floor and stretch your arms forward while your forehead rests on the floor. Hold the pose for five breaths. Now move your arms to one side so that the side muscles of your trunk are stretched. Hold for five breaths and then switch sides for four reps.
- Plank position with leg raises will work your core and engage your back as well.
- Lunges to stretch your psoas muscle (a core muscle that works on your hip joint) and relieve tightness and soreness.
- The bird–dog pose – Start on all fours and stretch alternate arm and leg. When you are in this pose your right arm will be stretched out in front and your left leg extended backwards. Hold for three breaths and

then switch. Repeat eight times. This exercise works on your lower back muscles.

e. After about five–six months after delivery, it is usually safe to take up any form of aerobic exercise such as jogging, Zumba or cycling. Since you will be pressed for time because of the baby, one great way to get a moderate impact aerobic workout is to dance in front of your baby. I used to make my little one sit in his rocker chair, put on some music and dance a whacky energetic dance. Babies are very happy to watch their moms dance at this age since they are not as mobile. If the baby gets restless you can take him out of the chair and bounce him in air and use him as a weight too! The baby will have adequate neck control by now, so you can hold the baby on your hip and do a simple slow stepping dance with him. This is an enjoyable workout as well as a great bonding activity for mother and child. The jumping and bouncing to the music are great for the baby's development and cognition as he picks on the rhythm and gets vestibular stimulation by the motion.

After six months

By now your body should have recovered and regained its previous strength. If you are returning to work, then your exercise routine will suffer too. Rather than going into a frenzy obsessing about your workout, adjust and compromise on it. Instead of half hour yoga sessions, go for twenty minutes. Schedule your workouts over the weekend.

An important thing to remember is that at six months, you will begin weaning your child and your breastfeeding frequency and volume will reduce as a result. Especially if you plan to rejoin work, you might scale back on day time feeds or pump. Either way your plump breasts will begin to sag a little because of the reduced volume of milk produced. Two important exercises at this time would be:

a. Hold a dupatta behind your back with both your hands and stretch it. Start at your lower back level and tug at the dupatta outwards with both arms. Hold the position for five breaths. Next hold the dupatta at the level of your shoulders behind you and tug. Similarly, hold the dupatta above your head and tug. This exercise works on your pectorals and improves the sag in your breasts. You can do this exercise in the bathroom without a bra on when you undress for your daily bath. Aim to do it for five minutes every day.
b. If you wish to reduce your milk flow during the day once you rejoin work, then practice walking up and down the stairs with your arms raised up. This reduces the blood and lymphatic flow of your breasts decreasing milk output and improves breast lift.

7

POSTPARTUM MENTAL HEALTH CARE

After delivery, the woman's mood disturbances are often oversimplified as hormonal changes. A hormone is a molecule that causes a series of reactions in our body and is important for functions such as fertility, metabolism, stress responses and immunity. If we attribute all our emotions to hormones, as is common these days, then we would be grossly unfair. The fact of the matter is that most things, if not all, suddenly change after delivery. Simple things a person takes for granted, such as food and sleep, are also unpredictable after delivery. The body undergoes an enormous physical stress during delivery and rather than getting adequate rest, it has to further nurture the new baby from the body's limited reserves. The rest and recreation which served as buffers to our daily life stressors and got us through to the next day are compromised.

Before I start breaking down post-delivery mood swings and postnatal depression, I want you to take a step back to see why you are on this chapter. If you feel you are getting thoughts of harming yourself or your child or feel that someone else is controlling your thoughts, then please seek immediate professional help. If you are in doubt about your own mental well-being, then look up the Edinburgh Postnatal Depression Scale online and take the test to see where you stand on the score. If you are in the depressed range, then do seek prompt psychiatric help.

The Importance of Buffers

A buffer is a person or a thing that lessens or moderates the impact of a change. In chemistry, we learned about chemical buffers and in our bodies, our blood serves to buffer the effect of what we breathe and what we eat to maintain our chemical equilibrium in a specific range. Our bank account is a buffer if we end up splurging on a vacation. Our savings take care of the extra cost we had to bear because of an episode of illness. There are buffer systems everywhere in nature and society. If we have an extra hard day, a good night's rest can restore our fatigued mental faculties and work as a buffer.

However, one's situation flips overnight when the baby is born. The upkeep of the household begins to unravel and so does the world of the couple. Taking care of the newborn is the longest journey one can undertake with an exhausted body and mind with no end in sight. Slowly all the buffer systems of the mother begin to deplete. The first of her resources to get depleted is her own strength. The woman has little energy to even comb her hair. The second of her resources to get challenged is her rest in every sense of the word. She has to sit and feed when she would love to lie down and forget the world in her blissful sleep. The new baby is dictating even the minutes she spends in the toilet.

For a mother who lives in the nuclear setup, precious time is spent on fixing her own meals. With sleep being so high on her priority, meal times often comprise of packaged food and boxed cereal rather than wholesome home-cooked foods. Her own body's nutrition resources get compromised over time because of breastfeeding and poor food intake. Low quality nutrition not only makes her prone to illnesses but also depletes the brain's reserves. Micronutrients such as iron, magnesium, zinc and vitamins that ensure the brain's chemical balance is maintained, are lost.

Lack of sleep is one of the most important factors that predisposes a woman to mood disturbances. One night of poor sleep leaves us groggy and cranky the next day. We have poor focus and it gets difficult to perform thinking tasks. For a new mother, broken sleep is the rule and the crucial regeneration of brain cells and brain connections which happen during our daily sleep is compromised. The prefrontal cortex – the area responsible for personality, complex thinking and decision making – is the most affected by lack of sleep. Aside from being irritable, one's short term memory as well as judgement is impaired.

Eventually, chronic lack of sleep could run into the course of depression or psychosis.

Another factor that can predispose a person to baby blues is chronic stress. Stress need not be a rough patch at work or a financial crisis. Simple things such as checking social media can be taxing. Adrenaline is the hormone that is produced immediately whenever there is a stressful situation. That is what is responsible for the heart racing and blood pressure rising whenever there is danger. In caveman times, that danger would be a real threat to survival such as a predator or a fire and the flight or fight response of adrenaline would remove us from the situation. What follows this surge of adrenaline is the slow rising hormone, cortisol. This hormone is slow to rise and slow to wane and has longer lasting effects on redistribution and storage of body fat as a mechanism to cope with mortal danger. In our modern life, simple events such as a lack of likes on our baby's photos can cause our hearts to race (because we get offended) as does peak-time traffic. Lack of social validation on Facebook and nasty feedback from our bosses leave us seething, but there is no need or place for a physical flight or fight response. Adrenaline spikes because of these emotional stressors and makes the cortisol levels rise too. Cortisol levels fall slowly. Repetitive adrenaline spikes due to stressors cause the cortisol level to stay up for longer and be at a sort of plateau level. We generally recover from the effects of adrenaline quickly but the more the cortisol accumulates in our body, the slower our body recovers from the effects of adrenaline. At first, when our adrenaline spikes, we feel sharper, wittier and fiercer but as we reel from its heady effect, we start to feel awful and have the figurative bad after taste from the experience.

Adrenaline and cortisol are both harmful for our brain regeneration in the long run. The effect of chronic stress is measurable in our brain. One of the starting points of depression is the accumulated brain cell death that has occurred in the event of adrenaline crash. The adrenaline rush is what gets us through the event. It is only after the offensive event is removed do we sustain the ill effects of stress hormones.

Most top movie stars who have battled depression and mental illness, have faced it at the peak of their careers after reaching success. The adrenaline rush of struggling for box office hits kept them going but once they reach the success they toiled for, they begin to stress down, and the adrenaline crash is what puts them in depression, pushing their fatigued brains in a downward spiral.

These days our entire pregnancy is a high stress event with more and more work. In the name of gender equality, we push ourselves to our limits without taking into account our physical state. The excitement and newness of the pregnancy makes us eagerly bide our time towards the grand finale of the perfectly planned birth of the baby. The delivery is viewed as a happily-ever-after but it is not going to be. There is a hard-hitting mind-numbing reality of routine and it is anything but exciting.

Why Baby Blues are on the Rise

The rise is quite obvious in India as the family structure is shifting from joint to nuclear and single motherhood. The lack of the woman's support system at home, or buffers, is what climaxes as postpartum depression and withdrawal. It wouldn't be farfetched to say that most women go through some degree of baby blues. Are the millennials a more fragile generation and cannot cope with the basic function of reproduction and child care? Quite the opposite actually.

Motherhood was a step up for the previous generation

Women from the generation of our mothers and grandmothers had a tough life after marriage. The daughter-in-law was treated inferior to every member of the family and was made to work like a slave. She had to not only adjust to a hostile environment but basic necessities of life such as food, rest and recreation were also rationed for her. If you ask any granny, she will tell you how her mother-in-law couldn't bear the sight of her resting and would rush to pile some work on her. She had to get up in the morning with the roosters and toil in this pre-machine period. There were no washing machines and no mixer grinders. Everything was done by hands, and might I add, the daughter-in-law's hands. She would be the last to eat dinner. Such was the life of our previous generation in most, if not all, joint families.

Yet, the last-generation-oppressed-daughter-in-law was better off. Since she had less education and self-dependence, she was so used to being oppressed that she made her peace with being neglected in her husband's home, but the birth of her baby gave her an identity and a position in the family. In addition, women were perceived as dispensable till they bore a child. A woman who proved her fertility solidified her status in society. Producing a child was an achievement in itself. And since she was always belittled without respite, the care, whatever little she received after motherhood, was a validation and an inclusion. An irrefutable promotion in the family hierarchy.

The double whammy for the present generation

With education and a push towards self-reliance under the banner of feminism, women these days have advantages their mothers were not entitled to. In a way, we have it easy because we don't have to push against the narrow-minded societal norms as hard as the generation before ours had to. We start at the top when we get married, so to speak. We now have more independence to choose our life partners and most of us start off in a nuclear setup with both husband and wife working. The modern-day strong-willed woman is the classical example of the type A personality. This personality is a temperament which encompasses ambition, competitiveness, focus on quality, need for control and an unrealistic sense of urgency as per the dictionary definition.

And to survive in this dog-eat-dog world, a woman has to have all these qualities to thrive.

In terms of living arrangements, the woman is on an indefinite honeymoon with her husband despite fights, work calls and no real honeymoon after marriage. She is her own master. She gyms, controls how she looks and is always at the top of her game. Once she conceives, planned or unplanned, her cherished body goes out of control. The kilos start piling and so do the deadlines. Excessive sleepiness, morning sickness and pregnancy-associated exhaustion slowly eat into her confidence as being an integral and indispensable part of the workforce. Then comes factoring in the maternity break and dealing with the perceptible shift in her status as the reliable employee. Once the baby is delivered, her worst nightmare – loss of control – comes to the forefront and that's when things can go downhill.

Loss of control and support

1. Loss of control and taking blame for all things not under one's control: When will the baby sleep and why the baby won't stop crying are puzzles we are far from decoding. It is something a mother cannot control as much as she would like to. Crying is how babies communicate everything and it takes time to figure out each baby's temperament and stressors. We have evolved in a way to accept blame. On the one hand, we know and feel miserable that we cannot decipher and control our crying child and on the other, we tend to take blame upon

ourselves for the crying which is beyond our control to start with.

2. Losing one's identity: When asked, Shikha always said she got married for kids rather than for companionship. So, it was no surprise that in a year and half after her wedding, she was blessed with her son. A smooth pregnancy and a rough postpartum later, she was yearning to hand over her son to a nanny and go back to work. Many modern-day women, just like Shikha, are lost after motherhood and pine to go back to the familiarities of their hectic work life and companionship with their husbands. We have learnt to enjoy the luxuries of investing time on ourselves and putting the needs of our bodies and ambitious fulfilments before anything else. The path to motherhood is paved with sacrifices and not a second goes by when you don't have to sacrifice something that you want or need for your baby. Shikha sought the help of her in-laws and joined work on a half shift in search of her old self. But one month down the line, not only did she find juggling work and home stretching her to her limits, she also realized her priorities and the sense of self-fulfilment had drastically transferred from her work to taking care of her son. You could be anywhere on this spectrum.
3. The need to belong to a community but the want for isolation: The rise of single parenting and nuclear families has prevented the smooth transition of a couple from spouse to parents. The woman used to

be surrounded by experienced mothers and could benefit from their expertise. The modern isolated family unit deprives the woman of the rite of passage to motherhood. Becoming a mother may be normal but the overnight flip of priorities, personality and her own life comes as a jolt. To have community support in such an overwhelming and draining time of life is not only suggested but rather imperative. The Westernized family setup not only undervalues but also trivializes the important and rather huge step into a new phase of life. The couple has to do everything alone and figure out the learning curve. They end up in a pit of frustration not knowing where to start, how to start or for that matter, what to start. Aside from needing a support system, there is bigger need of knowing that there is a set of reliable and caring people to fall back on.

Another way this isolation from the community affects a woman is at the level of the brain cells. Parts of the brain shrink when a person is in isolation which contributes to further damage to the mental health of the woman. Cultures that promote nuclear family and living in isolation have higher rates of depression as witnessed in the West and now in the evolving East.

4. Starting from scratch: A woman has to recreate herself once she becomes a mother. Her priorities change, her goals and aspirations too and her identity takes a 180-degree shift. In addition, there is an unspoken removal from the societal ladder where a woman used to

be a productive earning member of the community. Now she is reduced to an unkempt housewife and her role in the establishment she works for also gets jeopardized because of her priorities at home.

5. A lack of mentors and mentees: The relationship of wanting to accept information from our elders has been pretty much lost in the last two–three decades. We have outgrown wisdom fully and want to embrace the half-baked flow of information from the underdeveloped science of raising children that reaches us through the internet. Even if we do have all the resources and support, we don't wish to accept it from our elders whom we consider as ill-informed or less-educated than us. We seem to value information more if it comes from a dot com.
6. Oppression by poor body image: For some reason women expect to shed their pregnancy weight in no time. New moms are shamed by others and by themselves for their altered bodies. In this superfast world, we are all dying, and might I add killing ourselves in our haste to undo all the changes caused to our bodies in the process of conceiving and growing a child inside us.
7. Constant judgement: The most draining of emotional abuses is the constant nitpicking a new mother is subjected to. No matter how hard she is trying or how well she is handling the new baby, there will be some smirking matriarch passing snide comments at her perceived ineptness. The granny generation has little respect for the learning curve of the new mother and

spend their time criticizing the woman and discouraging her. I have dealt with the topic of the psyche of the matriarch in detail in the chapter on breastfeeding.

Ways to Stop and Reverse Mood Disturbances

1. Breastfeeding

One of the most important advantages of breastfeeding is the bonding between a mother and her baby. Such a solid foundation to a baby's relationship with the mother cannot be replicated by any dialogue or other activity. Sadly, the concept bonding is so abstract and non-tangible that it is often undervalued, and many a times completely overlooked.

To explain the importance of bonding, let me take the help of the institution of marriage. Non-consummation of marriage (no sex between the partners after marriage) is a ground for divorce. Only because men know the trauma of a sexless relationship has this issue found its place in our Constitution. A spouse (could be either the husband or wife) finds himself or herself victimized when his or her advances are ignored by the partner. Such is the importance of the human touch. Please note that not being able to bear a child is not accepted as grounds for divorce but rather lack of sex is. And because men have not been involved in the process of breastfeeding directly, patriarchy has kept silent about the need of the voiceless baby to be held and the importance of the mother to hold her child in order to fall in love with each other.

Without a doubt, the power a human touch can have over another human is undervalued. Have you seen how animals treat their young right after birth? They lick their young's body thoroughly and this is absolutely essential for the survival of the young. If rat babies are not licked by rat mommies, the babies die of urinary and digestive system failure. The stimulation in the genital region provided by the lick is necessary to initiate voiding of urine and faeces and development of other functions in the rat baby. In humans, the importance of being touched is often ignored and babies do survive even if not held and touched but being touched is only second in importance to being fed.

Yes, mothers are programmed to love their babies in theory but in practice the act of breastfeeding is what fosters this love. When you breastfeed, oxytocin is released. Oxytocin has multiple physical effects on the mother's body, but it also is the hormone responsible for feeling love towards this new unknown person who is keeping you awake at night and sucking out your body's resources. It takes a lot to love someone so selflessly and oxytocin is what's sowing the seeds of this lifelong attachment in the heart of the mother.

Breastfeeding mothers can take the exhaustion and sleep deprivation more in their stride than bottle-feeding mothers. The euphoria of falling in love is caused by oxytocin and so is the euphoria of falling in love with your exhausting newborn. Snuggling and cuddling with the baby happens more often after breastfeeding sessions, increasing the love and satisfaction from the relationship. The gratification a mother gets from breastfeeding makes up for all the selflessness she puts into raising the baby.

Oxytocin plays an important role in new mothers to cause them to forget the birth trauma, the misery of not sleeping for nights on end and the struggles of coping with a newborn's needs. Had it not been for this hormone's effect, not many mothers would ever agree to go through all the hassle to produce another child.

2. **Interactions with the baby:** *Daily massage and bath time*

Studies have shown that mothers stand to benefit a lot from touching their babies too. Women suffering from postpartum depression were taught to massage their babies and the effects observed. After a few weeks there was a noteworthy improvement in their mental health and the overall handling of their new lives as moms. Daily massaging and bathing the baby is an excellent low-cost way to get attached to your child and overcome the beginnings of baby blues.

3. **Interaction with the baby:** *Lullabies*

Live singing rather than recorded music has a positive effect on the feeding as well as sleeping patterns of a newborn. Babies who are sung to by their mother show better development in cognition. Lullabies need to come back in fashion. The lyrics of the lullabies tend to be simple and repetitive and the melody has a calming effect on the heart rate and blood pressures of both mother and child. These melodies have been associated with increased blood oxygen levels, oxytocin and endorphins levels, the possible prevention of potentially dangerous episodes of apnoea and low heart rates in babies. These can serve as a low-risk source of stimulation and reinforcement for increasing nipple sucking rates, providing infants with the nutrition they require for growth and development.

Lullabies are also the most successful type of music for relieving stress and improving the psychological health of a mother. They work as a vocational engagement for the mother and serve as therapy whether she is depressed or just plain low, increase milk output, calm her and help her get quality rest, and enhance parent–child bonding. The upcoming field of music therapy which includes singing and songwriting for the treatment of depression in adults has shown promise.

4. **Change your world view and thinking habits**

Women are more in control than they used to be, but this becomes a setback when it comes to motherhood. A new person is in the picture and most decisions are dictated by the baby's wishes. Things will spiral out of control and messes will be made. Now is the time to let go of the illusion of the multitasking superwoman and accept living in the moment. The mantra for sailing through motherhood is to take one hour at a time. Your life will not run as per schedule now that you have a baby in your life. Nor can you draw patterns from current behaviour and plan for the future. If your baby has slept in the afternoon today, he most likely will not tomorrow, so don't plan a soak in the tub for tomorrow just yet. Then again, if he bawled all night and you couldn't catch a wink, it doesn't mean there will be a repeat telecast today and you lose sleep dreading that! Most importantly, don't, just don't count the number of hours you haven't got to shut your eyes and fuss over that. Be mindful of the present and try to get things done on priority rather than spiral out of control trying to multitask and manage every single thing simultaneously.

5. **Stick to your rituals**

If your culture has naming or tonsuring ceremonies or celebrations marking the end of the postpartum period, then please do conduct them. They have stood the test of time because they mark significant transitions, your mind registers the important milestones and doesn't trivialize life changing events. Celebrate these milestones and recognize them as important. Soon enough your brain will catch up that child rearing is life-altering and that it's alright.

6. **Reclaim spirituality**

In most cultures, the woman abstains from prayer in her first forty days. Many women have found getting back to their daily worship and reconnection with a higher power liberating and empowering. The first month or two after delivery feel like the gloomiest period of a woman's life and being able to find spirituality gives her the hope and much needed patience to power her way through the phase. If you do not believe in prayer, then do give meditation a try. Nowadays there are meditation apps where one can listen to spiritual talks. These have done wonders for women battling feelings of hopelessness and loneliness in this taxing period.

7. **Find your support system**

Don't rely only on your partner for emotional connection and support. Reconnect with friends, find an online chat group for mothers to share your exasperations and lighten the load. It is exhausting to be engaged with the baby and live a life of social isolation. Perhaps not in the first month but do try to socialize after. It gives great relief in knowing you are not alone in your struggles.

8. **Wise usage of technology**

Joining online forums is like a double-edged sword. On the one hand you do get company, but it is also full of rubbish advice and has addictive potential. Most women these days lose precious sleep time by wasting hours online. Rather than giving their backs rest and closing their eyes, they get engrossed in checking their Instagram feed and updating Facebook. Social media is a big threat to the precarious sanity of a new mother because of the worth we place in 'the like button'. Also, seeing pictures of the unrealistic, unattainable bliss of others who are supposedly acing the parenting game is not great for the self-esteem of a new mother.

Caesarean Guilt

Nowadays, mothers face a new type of emotional trauma referred to as the caesarean guilt. More than one-third of the babies born these days are by operative deliveries. Advanced maternal age and inactive lifestyle can take just a part of the blame for this alarming trend but more of the responsibility rests with the healthcare system. More investigations and monitoring in hospitals lead to more interventions one might argue. Whatever the cause, women are not happy about giving birth the caesarean way.

We, as a race, have come a full circle in our relationship with science and technology. Only a few decades ago, we lapped up everything processed and embraced advances in science with open arms. Now, we have become increasingly wary of these man-made products and procedures and yearn to go back to our roots. Be it what we eat and how we raise our kids or even how we birth, we want to go au naturel. Consequently, women who haven't had the opportunity to birth vaginally are found feeling left out of the 'normal-birth-club'.

My first baby was born by an emergency caesarean. I had the worst of both the worlds – fourteen hours of fruitless labour followed by being cut open. I had a meltdown in the delivery room when I was asked to consent to a caesarean. The second time around I was all geared up for a VBAC (vaginal birth after caesarean). I did yoga, pelvic tilts, butterfly pose and even belly danced willing my baby to come out but she was quite happy inside and at forty weeks, with no baby in sight, my doctor and I had to give up and opt for a repeat caesarean. This time around, I was more relieved than crushed. I just wanted the baby out of me after my never-ending pregnancy and I knew that my doctor did her best at giving me a chance at a normal delivery.

My maid in particular was very invested in my birth stories and had a lot of expert opinion to offer. She would say that city girls can't tolerate pain so take the easy way out. And when I made the mistake of countering her and telling that it was an emergency because my labour didn't progress, she said, 'Yes, weak people can't tolerate labour pains, so they don't get labour pains'. I found myself offended by her ridiculous reasoning and partly defensive of my situation. In fact, most mothers who had been wanting a normal birth find themselves defending their doctor's decision and their own body's capability to give birth naturally.

For those of you who haven't been blessed enough to experience a natural birth, it's time to let go of this opportunity missed and count the blessing of having had the honour of becoming a mother. It is often perceived that caesarean moms are lazy or too scared to deliver normally. But we are in this situation for medical reasons rather than out of our own whim. Also, caesareans might seem like a breeze with no screaming, panting and pushing as a part of the process but it has its share of challenges. Caesarean is definitely not the easy way out because:

1. Having a needle inserted in your spine for anaesthesia is one of the most uncomfortable experiences ever.
2. While the anaesthesia begins to take effect, you get this horrible pins and needles sensation all over your lower body before you stop feeling anything.
3. The urinary catheter is a tube inserted into your bladder and can be painful during insertion. The pain is likely to be worse during removal.
4. Breastfeeding post-caesarean is very difficult. You can't turn to your side because you are paralyzed waist down for the first few hours after birth and trying to sit up sends shooting pains across the incision site.
5. Walking for the next few weeks feels like your gut is going to come spilling out of your incision. Even coughing and sneezing exert painful pressure on your stitches.
6. Recovery from caesarean takes longer than a normal delivery. There is a higher risk of caesarean site infection too. The delivery may seem fuss-free but our troubles actually begin after.
7. Subsequent pregnancies and labour become more dangerous and difficult after a caesarean.

Many mothers have attempted home births after their first caesareans because they were sure their doctor would do a repeat caesarean. While many have been able to give birth naturally with the help of a midwife, it would be unfair to say that what they did was right. Their resolve to avoid caesareans could put the life of their baby in danger. In fact, one patient refused a caesarean at all costs for her first delivery, putting her baby's life at risk and ended up giving birth to a stillborn child.

It's time we stopped judging our sacrifices and experiences and break free from society's judgement too. No birth is superior or inferior to another. Becoming a mother is not an exercise in martyrdom. Shaming new moms has become so rampant and being judged by other moms is worse for our emotional health than sleep deprivation or a bawling baby. We judge ourselves worse than anyone else does. Starting on this wrong note leaves us unforgiving of ourselves and we often label ourselves as 'bad moms'. Not being able to deliver normally leaves an empty emotional hole in our hearts and this concern of the new mother is often left unaddressed by her partner and doctor alike. I have gotten around to accepting my caesarean journey only after the birth of my second child. Even now when I am judged for not delivering normally, I just shrug it off but it's taken me years to reach this stage.

Speaking to many other moms who have had similar birthing stories has helped me. You could join an online community and anonymously vent about your experiences. Schedule an appointment with your doctor to discuss your birthing's detailed history. This will help you get closure with the events that occurred in the delivery room. Knowing in depth why there was no other way besides a caesarean would alleviate your sense of 'failure' to some extent. If you feel particularly haunted by your experience, then make sure you speak to an expert counsellor.

8

POST-BABY BEDROOMS

The Changed Dynamics with the Partner

After childbirth, the most common complaint the partner has is that his wife has changed. The change is more often a rude surprise rather than negative per se. A demure woman may have turned into an authoritative mother or an extrovert, outgoing personality may have become a more settled and sober one. These aren't bad qualities in a person. It's just different from what one was used to. In this day and age where people think it's their birth right to get life partners custom-made as per their choices, adapting to changes has become passé. Rather than embracing this newness in the next phase of our lives, we want to run for shelter in the familiarities of our past lives. To make this transition into parenthood easier for mothers and fathers, I would like to break down the processes occurring in the minds and bodies of new mothers to shed light on their new personalities.

1. **A woman has an overdose of touch sensation:** On a physical level, a woman has to endure so many new sensations from a strained back to sore nipples to pain in the stitches. Her skin receptors are running on max capacity transmitting sensations to her fuzzy, sleepy brain. The dulled mental capacity and overloaded sensory input makes her averse to any more physical touch, and more so, a sexually suggestive one. Your once sensual partner is now a perpetually annoyed person.
2. **An under deprivation of verbal communication:** Life changes within a day of giving birth and the change is a drastic one at that. The mother's social life is hit the hardest by the new arrival. We are experiencing so many things but don't have the time or avenue to talk to anyone about it. Parenting is mind-numbing drudgery and a high intensity challenge all at the same time. Our main mode of communication changes from talking to an adult to interpreting a newborn.
3. **Over stimulation by non-verbal cues from babies:** Over a short period of time, in just a few days, a woman begins to master the fine art of interpreting her newborn's cries, expressions and body language. At first, it is mind-boggling and terrorizing. As the weeks roll by, the mother learns to adapt to and understand the needs of her little baby. What starts off as a frustrating, one-way communication, soon turns into longer eye contact and brief acknowledging smiles from the baby. By the time the woman hits the six-week mark, she has tuned

herself completely into the baby's frequency and at a subconscious level finds it hard to communicate verbally alone. This applies more to intimate relationships such as that with her partner. When he talks to her while he absent-mindedly scrolls through his Twitter feed, he will get an alarmingly snappy reaction from her for not giving her his undivided attention. And there are more feuds over Facebook in households after the child's birth than you can guess. The woman now seeks validation and importance not through the mere physical presence of her husband but instead by meaningful eye contact and single-minded attention – just the way she communicates with her own baby.

4. **Patience and understanding reserves are sparse:** Sleep deprivation, fatigue and the physically taxing nature of the job of the mother leaves her with little patience and understanding for situations reeling out of control. The hormonal fluctuations add to the temperament without a doubt and so does raging hunger.
5. **The mounting baby obsessions:** Becoming a mother is a giant one-way trip to an unfamiliar uncharted territory and there is really no way back. Some women get homesick for the familiarities of the past and feel overdosed by the baby obsession. The loss of her personal space and sense of being is a rather overwhelming one because these days, me-time and my-space are given more importance than they used to. It is not wrong to want personal time and space but it's just a maladaptive

approach when it comes to rearing a child because inadvertently, we have to put ourselves second, and it is only a matter of time before that comes naturally to us. Mothers with difficult births and rocky post-delivery journeys especially resist putting their babies first and wish for the comfort zone that was their past.

6. **Delving into the obsessive mother role early on:** These women tend to have a fairly adapted motherhood and make the babies the centre of their universe early on. Such mothers don't have any emotional reserves for their partners. The partner often feels neglected but he needs to understand that his wife is truly giving her all to raising their child and instead of feeling neglected and undesired in the two-sided mother–baby equation, he should participate in their lives without a formal invitation. The man must slowly build on his role as the father and keep in mind that he might be a late entrant, but he is for sure the hero.
7. **Sexual non-concordance:** This term simply means your body and mind aren't on the same page. For example, your lubrication maybe fine but you are not able to get into the mood due to preoccupation with the baby. Or you feel aroused, but your body does not come on the same plane as your mind and does not physically respond. Aside from physical reasons such as fatigue and lack of sex hormones, the mind is always thinking about the baby and one doesn't get to fully relax. Women stop themselves from entering the realm of arousal just

because they fear that they might get interrupted during the act by the baby's cries. The brain is working overtime and finds it hard to slow down enough to want relaxation and recreation. Dealing with this problem will require more effort from the partner.

8. **The thanklessness cycle:** We have started off with golden stars in kindergarten and gone on to receive appraisals as employees. Being a new parent is the world's most thankless job. This glitch in the system of getting no appreciation or remuneration for such hard work is sensed and perceived but not vocalized by parents who toil after their newborns. You need to appreciate each other on behalf of the baby. Mothers need it more because they are the primary caregivers. So, 'Dear Parent, if your self-assured partner suddenly seems needy after becoming a mother, that's because she needs you to appreciate the effort she is putting into looking after your child. Be sure to listen to her problems and offer solace in the form of some appreciation as often as you can to keep her afloat.'
9. **The illusion of romance, spontaneity and butterflies:** This is one of the biggest pitfalls of this generation. Our brains have grown feeding on fodder from unattainable romances in movies and expect the adrenaline rush that we first had when we were dating our partners. Parenthood is the mighty adrenaline crash where all the excitement from pregnancy ends in the grungiest anticlimax ever. Becoming a parent anchors you to life.

There won't be fireworks to end your happily ever after but there will be projectile vomiting and blowout diapers to clear up in the after credits. I wouldn't say romance dies after a baby comes into the picture. It is as alive as you want it to be, but it is funnier and more familiar and less heart-skipping-a-beat kind. It would be wise to expect monotony, routine and sameness and take comfort in knowing you now belong to a family that your partner and you created together.

How to Get Sexy Time

For men first comes desire, then they get aroused and approach their partners. The opposite is true for women. First, they are aroused by their partners and only then do they sexually desire them. So instead of expecting a little touch and a mere five-minute-long foreplay to get you some intimacy, you need to work on the strategy of arousing your lady and getting her in the sexy zone. Think of it as a chance to court her all over again. Your partner is, in a sense, a brand-new person. Her body has changed dramatically as has her brain in terms of processing you. The lack of sleep, the hormones and the new baby have actually physically altered her brain. The rising oxytocin and waning sex hormones forge new neuronal connections in the brain mildly changing the woman's personality and demeanour.

Foreplay is now a day-long event. To get your hassled lady in the mood is often an uphill crawl. Sometimes it takes days of flirting and spooning with each other before you guys get any real time together to do the deed. That's okay too. Women cannot be turned on just like that. And mothers of small babies are especially harder to turn on because of the constantly working brain ticking off chores on her to-do list. At this point, I'll let you in on a secret. Nothing is sexier for a woman than her man desiring her and expressing that desire. So men, be flirty during the day via text messages. When you are at home, brush against her suggestively, cop a feel or give her a sultry stare to make her feel desired. Your spouse will feel sexier all day long and that may manifest in the bedroom at night.

It doesn't take sexy lingerie or handcuffs to get the heat up in the bedroom. Just by being polite to each other when tempers should be soaring (like when the baby is throwing a fit), you can turn your wife on. A sweet compliment and a caring gesture go a long way. Parenthood strengthens the couple's bond as they are thrown together in one team as parents. Just being there for each other at the end of yet-another-day as parents, brings you so much closer to one another.

Share the load

Men need to pitch in more daily to help out their wives. Yes, you may have a full shift and you need your recreation, but she is working 24x7 with the new baby and she deserves it. Make sure you change at least one diaper a day and take the baby away from her for an hour, so that she can enjoy a stroll or some trash TV. The initial days of motherhood are like a sentence of solitary confinement and slavery rolled into one. Give her a taste of lost freedom often by sharing responsibilities and doing more than your entitled male self is expected to do. An hour of uninterrupted sleep will give a world of difference to her mental state and could also get her in the mood.

Lower your expectations

I had pointed out that we millennials tend to hang onto the illusion of romance and think of it as our life-long right. The excitement of a new relationship is just raging hormones and once you find your mate, your body is going to adjust and adapt to it. There is something called the law of hedonic asymmetry in human nature. We tend to adapt to pleasure quickly whereas pain and discomfort keeps grabbing our attention. Just because the presence of your spouse doesn't flip your stomach, don't lose heart and think your relationship is failing. You have adapted to the presence of your mate at a physical level. It's time your mind adjusts to the idea of a familiar intimacy as well, rather than raging passion.

Giving the partner attention

As a mother and wife, I want to tell you that maintaining your relationship with your better half will take some effort. You cannot just wait for him to make the first move. Men often feel left out after the baby is born. The wives give so much attention to the babies and their own bodies require so much nurturing that the needs of the partner are often put on the back burner. You can treat your partner by making the first move once in a while. Men articulate their needs and emotions less and are often left wanting. To top it, they often don't even realize what they need. So, every other day, at least, discuss how things are going for each other. You will find yourselves speaking so often about only the baby, that your individuality will be pushed into the background. Women complain and say what's on their mind. And men will rarely, if ever, say that they need to talk but they do. Maybe your spouse is the stoic no-talker. Try to reconnect with him the way you and only you, as his wife, can. You will realize you both don't need titillation. Just a heart-to-heart conversation can sometimes get transformed to the strongest of passions.

What to Expect in the Bedroom

If you don't have kids yet, here is one thing to stop you from planning them, like ever! Kids have a state-of-the-art antenna to catch you doing hanky-panky. No matter how quiet you guys have trained yourself to be in the bedroom, the baby can sniff out your naughty doings and be alert. Many moms have had their six-month-old babies standing holding the railing inside the crib watching the mom and dad do it. It's like being raided by the police. Sometimes while putting the baby to bed if the dad suggestively brushes his leg against the mom's leg, the baby is alert and cries. After my first baby was born, my husband had begun his start-up and used to travel very frequently. I kid you not, but my son used to wake up and cry if my husband would even send a naughty text!

Science says that babies have this inbuilt reflex to stop mom and dad from getting it on by being a little extra demanding on 'those days'. It is in the best interests of the baby to not allow anything from happening and prevent a sibling from coming into his/her life and having to share mommy.

The romance isn't dead after having babies, now is it? Just for you ladies and gentlemen, I am going to bring to you top positions in bed after having babies.

The Top Positions in Bed after Having a Baby!

India is the land of the *Kama Sutra* and it reflects year after year in our population census. Mommies are exhausted, daddies are hassled, yet Indians churn out one baby after another after another. How? Well here is a peek into an Indian parents' bedroom to get to know their hottest positions!

The Incorrigible H!

Mommy on one edge of the bed, daddy on the other. Baby lying across horizontally touching papa with tiny fingers and nudging mumma with tiny toes. No matter how many times you align the baby with yourself, you will fail! It is the super popular H and cannot be corrected.

The 69 position with the capital 6!

Ever knew numbers could have capitals? Here is the latest parenting version of the super-hot 69 position. Mumma is the capital 6 and the tiny 9 is the baby who has somehow flipped in his sleep and whose feet have burrowed into the warmth of mumma's mouth.

The toe digger's magic

Toes are hot! And sweaty if they have been burrowing in your ribs all night long. This position goes together with incorrigible H and capital 69. Toes dig and scoop into your ribs, face and tummy. Getting sweaty yet?

Mission-eerie

A spin-off of the classic missionary position. Mission-eerie! The mission of the baby is to eerily pop up facing you. Millions of babies and parents can vouch for the fact that babies can never ever let you turn to the other side in your sleep. Like ever! Even if you ever commit the original sin of rolling over, you will either be punished like a naughty girl by your baby crying and clawing at your back. Or the baby will conveniently crawl over your body to end up on your other side. You can open your eyes to your phantom baby and be spooked out of your sleep!

The all-night twister

This position is sure to keep you up all night long. The tiny thing between you and your spouse twisting and kicking all night in his sleep is sure to keep you up for the better part of the night. And you can definitely get some action in this position. One kick in the jaw with a tiny-yet-surprisingly-powerful foot will surely steal your breath away.

The midnight course

Some babies just love to put their filthy hands in the comforts of their mumma's mouths during sleep. Right in the middle of the night, you can enjoy the salty-sweet grimy taste of wherever your rug rat's hands have been during the day!

The cliff hanger

You can have the biggest queen size bed but it can never contain all the passion that comes from within you, now can it? You may have given birth to a tiny kid but he passionately drives you to the edge of the bed. Leaving you precariously perched at the edge (with the rest of the expanse of the bed empty). Many a times your butt will be hanging out of the bed. Quite literally, the cliff hanger.

That being said, babies do have siblings. If the baby is tuned in to the parents' intentions, then even the parents have the *main bhi tera baap hoon* (I am smarter than you) attitude. After delivery there is the mandatory six-week period of abstinence. If all is good in your recovery and adjustment, then you can get back on track as soon as your postpartum period is over. Usually, there is no cut off or restriction on the number of times you do it or the positions you should favour but make sure you do get a thumbs up from your doctor before doing it for the first time after your delivery. Be particular to get your episiotomy stitches or your caesarean scar physically examined at your six-week follow-up with your doctor. Ask whatever is on your mind at your consultation. The doctor is a professional and will not judge you for your questions. If your health has been decent, then all positions are okay.

Here are some tips to get some rocking and rolling done with a baby in your lives.

1. **Be an opportunist:** Schedule your sexy time not at bedtime but on some other time of the day. You could do it when the grandparents are playing with the baby in the evening. Or when after playing in the park, your neighbour can take the baby home. Make hay while the sun shines.
2. **Get a partner in crime:** Maybe a friend of yours has struggled with a dry spell owing to her alert baby? She, for sure, will empathize with you. Have a date with your man by having your friend babysit for an hour or so. And you can always return the favour.
3. **Trick the intruder:** Most babies fall asleep on the breast and can smell their mom going missing even in deep sleep. Place your dupatta or whatever you were wearing next to the baby, keeping him/her warm and go get busy.
4. **Keep the baby safe:** Keep the baby in her crib while you get it on. Sometimes the baby will get up while you are in the middle of the act. As long as the baby is safe, you

can finish what you started. Most parents find it hard to continue if the baby starts crying for them. You can interrupt what you are doing, take the baby and put her back to sleep. Most experienced parents who have mastered doing it whenever and wherever, can pick up where they left off. Best way to not let the baby's crying be a mood spoiler is by laughing at the situation and not letting it get to you. Accepting your fate is an integral part of relatively smooth parenting. Those of you who enjoy the privacy of a nuclear family can use another room after having tucked the baby to bed and ensured his/her safety in case he/she gets up, but the ones in a joint family don't have such privileges and will have to make do in the same room.

5. **The adjustments for new moms:** Excited mothers can be leaky! Breastfeeding mommies keep your bras on if you don't want any leakage accidents. And especially during the first six months of breastfeeding you will find any above-the-belt action will make you leak more. Men, please be a little less handsy. Women, stock up on breast pads, particularly for those sessions.

   Also, breastfeeding causes vaginal dryness. It is not a cause for concern per se but can cause some discomfort during intercourse. A lubrication gel can take care of that situation very well.

6. **Cuddle and snuggle:** Sometimes you can substitute the act with just a little caressing and fondling. That is okay too. Most parents and especially moms are so

exhausted after the day that she barely has the energy to get in the mood. Cuddling with your partner and engaging in some pillow talk can be more rewarding on an emotional level than 'doing it'. You are more relaxed, can reconnect with your husband and share all that you both did during the day.

To IUD or not to IUD

After delivery, the birth control needs of a woman change. The pill contains hormones and hence not prescribed for the nursing mother as oestrogen, the main constituent of most pills, can be passed to the baby via breast milk. This hormone also decreases milk output in the mother. Oestrogen is for baby making, not baby feeding. Oestrogen rises and falls during the month and the change is what causes ovulation and conception. An uninterrupted steady dose through the month causes the contraceptive effect. During pregnancy, the placenta produces more of it to prepare the body for birth. Some mothers who so desire tablets for contraception are given low dose progesterone pill called the mini-pill but it is strongly discouraged in medical practice as we can never be absolutely sure of how much of the hormone reaches the baby through the milk.

In India, the medical practitioner is most likely to advise either condoms or IUDs. The safest non-invasive method for contraception is always the condom but most couples in long-term relationships end up opting for IUDs. The reason could be the lazy men not wanting to do any work or it could just be a matter of personal preference.

In this section, I want to debunk the shocking myths floating around IUDs in the mommy community. From laughable to plain idiotic, there are all sorts of 'facts' dished out by so-called experienced mothers and lapped up by the inexperienced ones. Knighting ceremonies are being performed to induct unsuspecting naïve mothers into the 'I-hate-copper T club'. No medicine or intervention is without its inherent risks and benefits. So here I present the case of copper T so that you can make an informed decision and not have your neighbour decide what's best for you.

Myth: An IUD causes a lot of bleeding

This is a half-truth. Every woman responds differently to copper T. Some women don't have a sigh escape their lips and can forget about the foreign body residing inside their uterus but other unfortunate ones could have heavy bleeding during periods, with bleeding between cycles which is followed by more period bleeding even before you throw away your last used pad.

No intervention has the exact same effect on every person. The most common scenario is mild spotting or a few days of light bleeding right after the copper T insertion. If you haven't begun your periods post-delivery then this will not cause any effect on your periods. Typically, your doctor will advise you to get copper T inserted 2-3 months after delivery. This gap is to make sure your uterus has retracted back to its original pre-pregnancy state. The bleeding following the copper T insertion is because your uterus is irritated, and the cramping and bleeding is an attempt to expel out the irritant. But in some women, the bleeding is so severe that she requires the IUD to be removed.

Reality: Copper T may or may not cause heavy bleeding. Even if it does, it is not a life-threatening emergency and can be removed without any long-lasting effects. You could give it a try and if things don't work out, you and copper T can go separate ways any time you wish. The opposite is true in the case of hormonal IUDs which reduce your bleeding over time. But as with any hormonal birth control it comes with its own profile of nasty side effects such as weight gain, cysts, breast pain and acne. In this regard, copper T gets a higher score as it does not affect your body's hormonal balance.

Myth: Copper T will cause your periods to come early

No. A copper T is an inert body with no effect on your ovulation. Just because you bled from your lady parts does not mean it is periods. You may encounter annoying spotting once in a while. In my experience, my periods were back four months after my first delivery and nine months later in case of my second.

Reality: A copper T will not cause your periods to come back early. A hormonal IUD on the other hand is recommended for women with heavier periods as it will reduce the bleeding severity.

Myth: Rough sex can dislodge a copper T

The copper T is not suspended mid-air. After it is inserted, the uterus views it as a foreign object and tries to expel it. At the same time your immune system is trying to launch an attack against the foreign body. The blood cells and uterine tissue entangle the foreign device causing it to be tethered to the uterus. So, can rough sex dislodge your IUD? Yes, it's a possibility but so can absolutely nothing. Just walking can expel the IUD from your body. There is no need to limit activity.

Reality: Copper T can get dislodged for any reason and not necessarily by activity.

Myth: Cramps are terrible because of copper T

This is again true in some sense but not a rule. After my first baby, for my first 3-4 periods I had nastier than usual cramps but later on, they settled. Some patients and women I know had such severe cramps and a heavy flow that they had to get the IUD removed. Even hormonal IUDs can cause more cramps.

Reality: Yes, you can get severe cramps for a few cycles, but it eventually settles. If you are one of the unlucky few whose cramps are vengeful, then speak to your doctor about removal and alternate options.

Fact: You can get pregnant with an IUD inside

This is unfortunately possible. Except for abstinence, no contraception is a 100 per cent effective. The failure rate of copper T is anywhere from 1–2 per cent. That means 2 out of 100 women can get pregnant while having copper T in them. Condoms have a failure rate of 3 per cent. It can be as high as 19 per cent if the condoms are improperly stored (in heat) or are expired. And copper T is more suitable for married couples and couples in long-term relationships as you don't have to think about protection in the heat of the moment or worry about running out of condoms. Hormonal IUDs will ensure you have fewer chances of pregnancy compared to copper T.

Fact: Copper T causes pelvic and yeast infections

This is supported by an overwhelming incidence of pelvic infections in women with IUDs. In fact, I had recurring pelvic infections with my first copper T. I had a dull, nagging cramp-like pain in my lower abdomen even after my period would get over. I would feel ill but had no severe symptoms such as high fever or excruciating abdominal pain. Don't expect any pus-like discharge or a spiking fever. It is just an annoying infection hanging out in your uterus. A course of antibiotics, some painkillers and abstinence for the duration of antibiotic course should solve the problem.

The foreign body serves as a focus for holding onto bacteria and hence the recurring infection. The threads of the copper

T also serve a focus for infection and that explains the higher incidence of yeast infections in women using copper T.

Because I had recurring pelvic infections with my first copper T, the second time around, my doctor advised copper T with silver coating on the arms. The silver has antibacterial properties and prevents infections. With my second copper T so far, I have been pelvic infection free.

Reality: A true fact. But it is not a monstrous infection. A copper T with silver coating is a good option for those getting recurring infections as the silver ions have antibacterial properties.

Fact: Copper T hurts

Insertion of copper T can be painful no doubt but just because it's a metal being inserted does not mean your gynaecologist is stabbing you. I was amazed when someone I was counselling to get copper T, to space her kids, said it is sharp and would hurt.

The conversation with her got me writing this chapter. I later spoke to her over the phone and got all her misinformation (regarding immunity, pain) corrected. She was sitting on to compile all these myths for my chapter. She is one slacker when it comes to protection during intercourse and is certainly not one to practice abstinence! So, a whole lot of convincing was needed to avoid any more 'accidents'. Her two back-to-back pregnancies had really drained her physically and I was scared that she would get pregnant again because of misinformation.

Reality: An IUD per se does not hurt. The speculum might be uncomfortable depending on your state of being relaxed and your pain tolerance but if you have delivered a kid (caesarean or normally), then you are pretty badass and can take this for sure!

My experiences with copper T

After my first delivery I had returned to work fairly early at three and a half months. So, one such day I was at work and popped into my OBG's office just to greet her. I casually asked her while chatting when would be a good time for me to get the copper T inserted. She replied, 'I am free after this patient. You want to do it now?'

'Okay, sure,' I replied.

I went and prepped the minor OT and supplies for the copper T insertion myself (it was close to lunch hour so I was free). On the way to my OPD, I called up my husband to inform him about the procedure. He was pretty freaked by the sudden announcement and promised to come to the hospital as soon as he could get out of his meeting. After seeing a few more patients, I went to the OT to get my procedure done.

The insertion wasn't bad but it wasn't a walk in the park either. The doctor used a speculum to see if my cervix and everything else was healthy. The insertion felt like a blow in my gut. Like someone kicked the wind out of me without actually kicking me. Other than that, the procedure was quick and hassle-free. After it was done, the doctor comforted me and asked me to lie down for a few minutes. My husband had reached the hospital by then. He had got me a sweet lime juice and looked so sweet with worry on his face. I had to comfort him saying that I was all right and sat with him for ten minutes after recovering from the insertion. After the juice, I felt a lot better and I went back to seeing my patients.

I am not narrating a tale where I am a superwoman and I can get back to work within fifteen minutes of getting a copper T inserted. Just because I was well-informed about copper T and did not make a huge fuss about it, I could get it done like it was no big deal. Some women aren't as lucky. They bleed after the insertion or are over sensitive to the speculum insertion. A woman needing to rest for the remaining day is not a sign of weakness or drama. That person just reacted differently to it.

The sequel

After my second delivery I had two new matriarchs to oppress me in a completely different way from my first. Let's just skip the sob details of my ordeal (because tough situations can arise for everyone). Suffice it to say that I was treated like a lower mortal whose only purpose was to cater to their whims and fancies. It was a sort of imposed slavery with undercurrents of emotional torture. They engulfed my home with a strange vibe of hostility and made peaceful living a tad difficult. I always wondered when the next jibe or taunt would come and which one of the two is upset with me (for no apparent reason).

The flow of guests to visit the baby was endless so one day I just went to get a check-up and get the IUD inserted by myself, baby in tow. As soon as I reached the hospital, the nurses and staff gushed over my adorable baby and focused on my fat hips. Every second person commented on how I had gotten fatter post-delivery. By the time I reached the procedure room I was battered by the nasty comments and had peaked into full throttle self-pity mode. I was mentally listing all the pettiness and meanness I was subjected to and how much I was made to suffer for no good reason. So, when my doctor (with whom I share a very friendly banter sort of a rapport) cracked a tiny joke at my expense (no she did not call me fat), I burst into tears. I was in a vulnerable position with my legs on stirrups being prepped for the procedure and I was raw from all the bullying and insults. Her joke was the straw that broke the camel's back.

I immediately closed up my legs, sat up and started sobbing. Both the doctor and nurse were stunned to get such a reaction from me. She understood something bigger was bothering me and comforted me and asked what was happening in my life. The flood gates had opened, and I cried and complained to my heart's content. She consoled me and cursed my tyrants. I felt a lot better after the weep fest.

True to its form, the copper T knocked the wind out of me this time too. I had borne it with as little as a gasp the last time around. But my fragile emotional state did not let me take this stress well. It was very painful this time. My baby was downstairs with one of the nurses and was bringing the hospital down crying for me. After the insertion, I did not even get to lie down for a bit as I rushed downstairs to nurse her. I was parched from my own crying and the procedure. And this time there was no lime juice waiting for me. The breastfeeding made me thirstier. I silently shed tears of misery, bled on the gauze in my underwear and nursed my daughter.

What to Expect in the Procedure Room

No two women are alike. Their medical histories, labours and deliveries are all different. Their pain tolerance and even rapport with family members as well as her doctor affects how she perceives this procedure (or any procedure for that matter). I shared my stories so that you can be prepared and make an informed decision. Many women I know had to get their IUDs removed because of the heavy bleeding they experienced. Even though I have always been among the unluckier ones in the period department (bad cramps, heavy flow lasting full seven days, and the works!), I was lucky with the copper T. I did have more cramps for a few months during my first two days of periods and a comparatively heavier flow, but it settled few months later.

For those of you leaning towards IUD, here is what to expect during the procedure:

1. The procedure will be conducted in a minor operation theatre/procedure room.
2. No anaesthesia (local or general) is required.

3. You will be made to lie on your back with your legs on stirrups.
4. A sims speculum will be inserted into your vagina to visualize your cervix and uterus.
5. The doctor will insert a slender, metal rod-like instrument to measure the depth of your uterus. It is called the uterine sound.
6. Then she will insert the copper T in a hollow plastic applicator and according to the measured depth, insert the applicator into your vagina and up into the uterus. She will then push the lever and the copper T will be lodged in your uterus.
7. The copper T has two threads made of a twine-like plastic. These threads are for assessing whether the copper T is in place. She will cut it high up in your cervix and leave it there. You cannot feel it hanging out of your vagina nor does it interfere with intercourse. In case you do get abnormal pain or discomfort due to the IUD then be sure to get yourself checked. An IUD could embed in your uterus wall and pierce it but that is an extremely rare complication.

For any IUD insertion, make sure to take an appointment after your periods have ended or if you haven't had your periods be sure it is around the date you expect it. During periods, the cervix is slightly dilated making the insertion easier and you can be sure you aren't pregnant.

9

MATERNITY BREAK

With the new era, gender roles are getting blurry and the gender divide practically non-existent. Notwithstanding the fact that we are in charge of the uterus and bearing babies, mother and father both contribute to rearing babies in today's evolved family structure. The father is not any more the sole breadwinner and many families take a call as to who should work after a baby is born taking into account total earnings and insurance benefits. It isn't surprising that some fathers these days have taken the nurturer's role and the mother is the hunter or gatherer so to speak.

Where lines of societal norms are getting blurred, the concept of maternity break also becomes a wee bit redundant. In more progressive countries such as The Netherlands and Sweden, family breaks are given instead of the singular lump of maternity break as seen in India. If you think practically, in a nuclear family, a woman cannot get by alone looking after herself and the baby especially in the first few weeks. She needs to focus on herself and her baby and try to get as much rest as possible and not worry about the dishes and ordering diapers. When everyone wants to stand independently on their own feet, there is not much of a backup support system in place in the tiny nuclear setup.

When the Indian parliament increased the paid maternity break from twelve to twenty-six weeks in 2017, women rejoiced in the country but only temporarily. When the buzz of this bold change wore off, did we come to realize that this supposed blessing was a curse for gender equality. Women were seen as a liability in the company, someone who would get knocked-up and leech resources from the business for six months. And to prove themselves as worthy of being employable and an asset in the workplace, more women rushed to rejoin work and prove their usefulness within a month or so after their deliveries. Weeks of paid maternity leave lay wasted as new mothers scurried to join back the rat race that their corporates were.

I am a feminist but I do not believe in gender equality. For as long as women have to bear children in their wombs, the genders cannot be equal. We have a mighty responsibility placed on our shoulders by nature. If we could share our baby-bearing burden with our partners, we would do it without thinking but as for now, as our worlds and families shrink, and our duties expand in this disconnected family unit, parental leave and not maternity leave is the way to go. I say this because:

1. Women get to have the rest they require if her partner is there at home full-time to support her without worrying about the added cost of having a new member in the house.
2. Even though the genders are not created equal, the burden of the way employees are viewed in the workforce, as a liability or an asset, is equalized if parental leave comes into force.
3. In the nuclear family, where duality in earning is the norm and many a times even a necessity, duality for baby care is also required. A woman cannot, and should not, be expected to care for the baby all by herself with scarce support for breastfeeding and childcare. If the baby or mother fall ill, the father is often the only support they have to fall back on. When the father is there to assist the mother in her breastfeeding journey, which is often an uphill one, she has better chances of succeeding.
4. The long-term benefits of breastfeeding and increased mother–child bonding put to shame the short-sighted view corporates seem to have about paying the mother for six months. Take obesity for example. Breastfeeding has a protective effect on the child against obesity. To put matters in perspective, look at the number of children suffering from childhood obesity. Decreased breastfeeding is to be blamed along with long hours of sitting and engaging with gadgets. The US spends billions on healthcare of obese adults and the cost is just rising with the diseases associated with obesity.

Paid maternity leave is a great start to a new life and has more far reaching consequences on the lives of the mother and child. And if we take away from every mother's life this essential need, then we stand to disrupt hers and her child's life for many years to come.

The 'Why' of It

Maternity breaks support breastfeeding. If the child is fed at the breast for the first one year, then the entire community and country stands to benefit from it.

1. Perfect food for the baby

Breastmilk provides the perfect balance of proteins, carbohydrates, fat, water and electrolytes for the baby. The composition of breast milk is perfectly suited for the newborn. It has the ideal composition of nutrients which will get absorbed maximally from his immature gut.

The lactose in the mother's milk is the best fuel for the baby and ideal for his brain development. The fatty acids present in the milk gives him a great start to a healthy heart. There are abundant factors in the mother's milk which helps in coating the small intestine of the newborn. The newborn's gut is poorly developed and needs the protective factors present in the milk. That is why it is advised to exclusively breastfeed up till six months. The baby's intestine is leaky, and any foreign food introduced before five or six months will sensitize the body abnormally to it. This sensitivity manifests as an allergic reaction to the same food in the future.

The kidneys and liver of the baby have to work less hard to process the mother's milk when compared to formula feeds. The baby's organs are still under development and need the gentle nourishment of the mother's milk rather than the strain of processing formula out of the body.

2. Provides the baby a solid foundation for his immunity

The colostrum is absolutely vital for the baby to get his source of Immunoglobulin A from the mother's milk. This antibody protects the child from future episodes of diarrhoea by giving it a headstart in building his immunity.

Lactoferrin and lactalbumin are the whey proteins in the human milk. They provide protection against deadly bacteria such as salmonella and E. coli. The whey protein in cow milk is betalactoglobulin which sadly promotes the growth of these deadly bacteria in the baby's gut.

There is a super long list of anti-infective factors in the mother's milk which are impossible to replicate by formula manufacturers. Interleukins, tumour necrosis factor, pancreatic secretory trypsin inhibitor is just the tip of the iceberg. All of these work together to promote the healthy development of the baby's gut as well as body.

The bacteria present in the infant's gut is supposed to produce Vitamin B12 and Vitamin K and provide protection against other harmful bacteria. The acidity of the human milk promotes optimal growth of the good bacteria. In addition, there are certain sugars in the mother's milk called oligosaccharides which provide sustenance to the good baby gut bacteria – Bifidobacterium infantis. The oligosaccharides in the mother's milk work as a prebiotic. (A probiotic is a beneficial micro-organism in your body. A prebiotic provides food for this good bacteria.)

In addition to a range of immune factors breastmilk contains, breastfeeding promotes the baby's thymus. The thymus is the organ responsible for processing a type of white blood cell. It is the largest in size at infancy and gradually shrinks. Breastfed babies' thymus shrinks slower when compared to bottle-fed babies. The factor responsible for this is not yet discovered. This is another way breastfeeding promotes immunity.

3. Promotes good eating habits and development of mouth and jaw

The composition of mother's milk is such that babies seldom overfeed. Also, breastfeeding on demand rather than formula feeding by the clock ensures we respond to hunger cues rather than feed him as a response to our own whim. This builds the foundation of a life of eating sensibly and not to a point of numbness. This eating pattern also protects the child from developing obesity and eating disorders in the future.

On the other end of the spectrum, babies fed on a schedule dictated by the mother rather than their own appetite are often left frustrated between feeds if hungry. Their hunger is disregarded because by the clock they shouldn't be fed just yet. I completely discourage the practice of feeding by a timetable. Growth spurts, increased activity and varying speed of digestion through the day means earlier or later demand for milk. They cry and get frustrated and are fed maybe half an hour later. Food for them then becomes a source to reduce this frustration of being fed late. This changes the brain's development pattern where food is seen as a source of comfort rather than nourishment, giving rise to the epidemic of comfort eating and eating disorders.

Aside from the goodness of milk, the act of sucking from the mother's breast itself is physically promotive of good oral development. The jaw of bottle-fed and pacifier addicted babies is narrower compared to the jaws of breastfed children. This structural impairment can lead to requiring dental alignment procedures later on, along with snoring and nose block problems in adulthood.

Long-term Benefits

1. Protects against future obesity

The cost of health care for the obese goes into billions in the US alone. Breastfeeding lays the ground for healthy optimal nutrition for the body's cells. It is nutrients delivered to the cells in amounts as required by the body. Formula milk comes nowhere close to breastmilk in this realm and especially promoting feeding by the clock is just mindlessly stuffing the baby and disrespecting his body's needs.

2. Insures against allergies

Formula milk is based on soy or cow milk protein. Exposing the infant body to these proteins so early in life is dangerous for the future health of the baby. The infantile gut which is still in the developing phase and a tad bit leaky allows for these foreign proteins to leak through and trigger an immune response to it. This allows for soy allergies and lactose intolerance in the future. The mother's milk, on the other hand, has such a composition that it coats the baby's intestines and provides the baby's gut with all the nutrients he needs in an easily absorbable form. In fact, breastmilk provides nourishment to the good gut bacteria whereas the proteins present in formula milk allow for the harmful bacteria to flourish in the gut. The burden of food allergies in the US is above $25 billion a year in addition to the $18 billion spent on other forms of allergies.

Early separation of mother and child is another reason why kids can get allergies. A baby who is breastfed gets the benefit of all the nutritional substances which protect the immune system. The stress hormones, that the mother passes onto the baby through her milk, shape the immune system as well as personality of the child. A mother who is supposed to join work early is more likely to introduce the bottle to get the baby adapted to it. The baby inhales the mother's stress hormones that she secretes in her sweat during their closeness during feeding. When the child is separated from his mother in day care, the formula milk is there but the protective effect of adrenaline that the child was used to inhaling while being fed by the mother is absent. This scenario is one of the first incidents of a full-on allergic attack.

Besides allergies, rates of even autoimmune diseases (diseases in which one's body attacks its own healthy tissues), such as coeliac disease, are less in breastfed babies.

3. Lesser divorces: An early start to meaningful adult relationships

In the West, from Day 1, the baby is made to sleep alone in his nursery. Being left by the parent to comfort himself in his colour-coordinated nursery is sort of criminal. Children who are held and comforted when they cry, grow up to have strong ties with their mothers and are able to replicate such relationships with their future spouse. Not getting closeness and comfort in infancy makes the person frustrated. On the primal evolutionary level, a person in stress has flight or fight response on being stressed in the short-term. But the subconscious reacts to the stress over long periods of time as a threat to his survival. So, in the long term the person tries to ensure survival of his lineage. What does this translate to? This thought process initiates behaviour where a person is seeking to continue his lineage with multiple sexual partners. Prolonged stress from infancy due to not being held plus weak bonds with the mother makes the person what we now call commitment-phobic. These children who grew unattached to their mothers are more prone to opting for multiple partners. Such is the effect of what you did with your child when he was a newborn. The more we keep our children at an arm's length and let them sleep alone, abandoned in their fancy cribs and separate nurseries, the more we are contributing to the crumbling of the institution of marriage.

4. Contributes to mother's well-being

Breastfeeding for longer protects the mother from ovarian, breast and uterine cancers. It also has a protective effect against postpartum blues and depression.

Breastfeeding, no doubt helps in weight loss, but the targeted fat is very specific in its case. The deeper abdominal fat that coats the internal organs – the visceral fat is what is shed by breastfeeding. Excessive visceral fat is what is responsible for clogged arteries, high cholesterol, diabetes and heart attacks. Research done on mothers seven years after the birth of their kids showed that those who had breastfed for four months or longer had lesser visceral fat when compared to mothers of the same overall weight who had breastfed for a shorter duration.

The Tumultuous Emotions of a Working Mother

It is hard to be a stay-at-home mom. For the mother who is used to being out and about conquering the world, this is nothing less than captivity. Even if the woman can afford to not earn, just staying at home with just a baby for company who doesn't talk and wearing clothes that don't flatter, is a big downer. We cannot be compared to our mothers' generation because our mindsets are different. Right from childhood, we grew up knowing that our place in the world is outside the house and not confined to the kitchen. We find fulfilment not in clearing cobwebs and ironing laundry but instead in scheduling and troubleshooting. The flip of personality comes down rather hard on us and to keep our own sanity we might need to go back to work. To maintain a balance for both yours and the baby's health, there are some preparations you can do beforehand. Discuss with your colleagues during the last trimester a mutually agreed-upon arrangement and work on projects from home a month or so after delivery. It will help you maintain your standing on the corporate ladder and not become irrelevant at the workplace. In fact, returning from your maternity break will also be easier as you wouldn't have lost touch with what has been going on at your workplace. Take up projects few weeks post-delivery that you can work on while at home. It is mind-numbingly boring to play peek-a-boo for the 100th time in the day and find fulfilment in the conversation that revolves around the baby's poop colour. A conference call or two during the work week can keep you in the loop and help you remain productive.

Rejoining Work

Depending on where you work, your maternity leave may vary anywhere from four months to a year. In my opinion every company must give a maternity break of a minimum of nine months to the woman and a one month fully paid paternity leave to the father. A better alternative, but a far cry as of now, is a lumped family leave where both parents can claim the leaves but sadly, mothers are not making these rules and the patriarchy will continue to disappoint us till we take the legal route and make the laws ourselves.

For every mother, the day she has to rejoin work is filled with apprehension, excitement, dread and what not. There is a roller coaster of emotions that she is riding on. She may be excited to be finally getting out of the house and reclaiming the role of a bread winner. She is filled with dread for leaving her little one alone in the care of a nanny or baby's Nani. She has a sense of losing the exclusive rights to the baby and gaining the freedom that she once had outside of her home. Restarting work is truly an overwhelming time. Once the schedule is set and the baby and mother adjust, it is back to dreary work days and Monday morning blues but the transition of 'back from the maternity break' is nothing short of excitement for first-time mothers.

Here are a few things that you need to truly mull over before you take the big leap back to work:

1. *Is right now the right time?*
   Maybe your baby is too young? Maybe you don't want to pump and feed and want to wait a few more months before you leave your precious child. Explore the opportunities your workplace is willing to offer you. Can

you extend your maternal sabbatical without much harm to your career? Perhaps you need to get out there right now to get your finances back in shape? Explore all these questions. Take your boss into confidence. Discuss your future in the company with him/her. Ask for better and more flexible timings. You can probably start off at the end of six months with a half shift. Maybe take up full day once your baby turns one. There is no rule book for how long you need to work for. Talk to your employer and figure out a schedule you are most comfortable with.

2. *Where will the baby care happen?*
Does your mother-in-law live with you? Is she fully supportive of your work and willing to completely take care of the baby? Most grannies are too old to be looking after a tiny yet energetic child. You can probably hire a maid-cum-nanny to primarily look after the baby under your mother-in-law's supervision. A friend of mine used to drop her son to her mother's place each day. The commute was a pain but then it was all worth it for her to watch her little one blossom under his Nani's wing.

Perhaps you don't have a grandparent around to help out. Look at the day care options around your workplace. You can just stand outside the day care and find out a lot about the day care by talking to the parents dropping off their kids. They can be super helpful. You can read parent reviews online. Find out about open door policy and CCTV camera facilities in day cares. I am wary of day cares that don't let parents walk in any time of the day. What is the super secret activity that you are engaging my little child in? Trust a creche or day care with open doors rather than ones that don't allow parents to walk in whenever. In today's growing day care industry, CCTV cameras are found in pretty much every day care facility. Some even have mobile apps that you can use to keep an eye on your kid's activities any time of the day by simply watching the live feed on your mobile.

3. *Figuring out the work schedule*
You cannot be rigid about your work schedule or about your baby's feeding schedule. Be mentally prepared to deal with good days and bad days – great pumping sessions and worrying pumping sessions, a happy baby and a tantrum-throwing baby, depending on the day, and sometimes multiple times in the same day. Two key qualities one should be armed with to take on breastfeeding as a working mother are flexibility and patience.

While you are willing to be flexible, be aware of your rights and expect a certain degree of flexibility and adjustment from your workplace as well. Maternity break laws are made by men and there is a dearth of mothers in the legislative panels formulating work laws but as the feminist wave is engulfing the workplace and more power is handed over to women, we can expect more from our workplace. Usually it is hard to have the breastfeeding conversation before delivery. Partly because until you have held and fed your child, you will not find enough gumption that only comes from being a mother or probably because you are not aware practically of all your needs as a breastfeeding mother.

Some of the things you can work out with your boss:

a. **Check the scope for work from home.** You could have a schedule where you reply to client emails and prepare proposals from home in the morning hours. You could drop in mid-morning and work till mid-afternoon. The rest of the emails and stuff that you can do on your laptop or phone, can be scheduled after you leave work.
b. **Instead of having a five-day work week, request a four-day work week.** So, work Monday, Tuesday and take off on Wednesday. Then get back to work on Thursday, Friday and then comes the weekend. This way you won't be away from your child for more than two days at a stretch.
c. **Request a pumping room.** This might be a hard one but it's definitely worth a shot. The common pantry can have a small cubicle with a couch, a table and a plug point. That is pretty much all you will need. If you have a cabin, then that's great too! Be sure to lock the door with a sign outside so as to not be disturbed and if the cubicle has glass around, get a laminated sticker to make sure it's not see-through.

d. You can **work for longer shifts** three-four days a week rather than working the smaller shift five days a week.
e. If you feel you can change jobs to a more favourable one like your own start-up, where you can work from home, then that would be ideal. For example, I started writing this book when my child was four months old. I had the itch to be gainfully employed but I refused to leave my kid and go back to seeing patients so soon. Now I feel like I have shifted the lanes of my career and am pleasantly surprised by my new vocation. However, give your new work from home the respect and discipline of work. I ensure I sit for a few hours at a desk and type and keep giving myself deadlines to finish my work. I do my research the rest of the day while breastfeeding or while the kids play in the park but I make sure that the morning hours are for compulsorily churning out words.
f. Some of the super large work firms have dedicated attached day care centres. Take advantage of that but be sure to ask for breastfeeding breaks (request a twenty–thirty minutes break). Please do realize that this break is something that should be your right and don't accept is as alms. Most cigarette–coffee breaks taken by office-goers at least twice a day last for the same amount of time! So, your demand is not particularly outrageous.

4. *Figuring out the feeding schedule*

   Every mother is different, and I cannot possibly deal with all the job variations and sitter arrangements. But I will try to help you out with different scenarios nonetheless. You can work around these points and figure out your own schedule:

   a. **Start the day late and end early**

      If your work requires you to be there from nine to five, then see if you can start your day at eleven and end at four. Work out a deal where your work presence online begins from around eight and you can manage the presentations, meetings and client face-to-face time during your presence at the workplace. Feed your baby at around 10:30 a.m. before dropping off your baby at the day care or with the sitter. If the baby is older and has started solids, then plan a solid meal around 12:30 p.m. followed by a nap. Most likely only one bottle of your pumped milk can be given at around 3 p.m. before you pick up the baby at 4 p.m.

   b. If you are sticking to your nine to five schedule, then breastfeed once as soon as you wake up, then once at drop off time. Pump mid-morning, at lunch hours and late afternoon. Make sure your pumped milk is stored as one-time feeds (preferably 60 ml or 120 ml milk servings). By the time you pick your baby at 5 p.m., he/she should be fed at the breast. I would advise you to feed the baby at the day care rather than in the car because you will get a chance to help your baby associate the creche with familiarity and comfort rather than a prison. You also get a chance to meet all the germs your baby had been hanging out with and give your body the opportunity to churn out antibodies for the bad guys your baby has slathered on his hands and body.

c. If pumping isn't working out for you and you want to opt for formula in his time at the creche, then here are a few things to keep in mind:
   - Breastfeed in the morning before dropping off the baby.
   - You need to pump at least once or twice during work. Even if you want to pump and dump, do it to keep your milk supply up.
   - If your baby is fairly big then you can scale back on your milk production and decide on weaning with one bottle of formula but do not resort to formula for the rest of the day when the two of you are together. The baby needs to feel comforted for the time he was away from you and missing out a feed here and there will stealthily reduce your milk production.
   - Solids can be given as the first feed after he is dropped off. The next feed will be post nap and that can be a bottle of formula. Then add another solid in the late afternoon. By evening, it will be time to see your baby. Be sure to inform the sitter

about your arrival lest they feed him after the two-hour interval. In case you are running late, ask the sitter to give a small feed but it is best to have a hungry baby at pickup time to relieve you of your engorged breasts.

5. *The importance of night-time feeds*

The baby's secure world of only 'mommy and me' is turned upside down by the work week. Make up for the time away from the baby by feeding more often in the evening and at night. The baby will not only latch on for food but will also need to compensate for the mommy smell and warmth he had missed out on all day long. And the more he sucks at night the more you make sure your milk production doesn't drop off one month after you start work. The reduction will be so insidious that you won't even be able to put your finger on when it happened.

Co-sleeping is a must for a successful night-time feeding routine. The presence of the baby next to you will ensure your hormones are working overtime without you even knowing. Also, as I have said earlier, baby's night-time feeds are not that hard on the mother. You barely have to wake up to feed. After a few months of sleeping with each other, the mother and baby know what is to be done in their sleep and a little bit of adjustment when the baby stirs will put the breast right into the baby's mouth.

Prolactin, if you will recall, is the milk producing hormone. Most hormones follow some sort of pattern of production. Many peak in the middle of the night during your restorative sleep. Prolactin is one of those. So, feeding during the night actually ensures you get aligned with your body's natural rhythm.

I hope this book has helped ease some of your worries about motherhood. Don't stress over situations and go with your instincts and you will be golden.

Happy Motherhood!

EPILOGUE

Being a Mother in the Times of Covid-19

The Covid-19 pandemic is an evolving topic and the research is still not 100 per cent conclusive. But if you have conceived during this pandemic and would like to retain the pregnancy then you should. *There is nothing to be scared of.* From experiencing H1N1 to dengue infections in pregnant women, I have not witnessed a change in the care provided to expecting moms. That being said, with Covid-19, there is a high risk of catching the infection from a hospital visit. The severity of the Covid-19 infection in pregnant women is not higher than the regular public but we cannot discount the mental stress an expecting woman and her family would go through because of Covid-19. It is better to be cautious. Here are a few tips that may prevent you from contracting this infection during your pregnancy.

Ways to Reduce Covid-19 Risk during Antenatal Visits

1. *Follow the regular precautions for any hospital visit:* Wear a facemask, maintain social distancing from the hospital staff and other patients and wash hands or use a handsanitizer.
2. *Be prepared for your visits:* One way to minimize the number of antenatal visits is getting clarity on what to expect in the next visit from your doctor. If there is a blood test needed, then get that done and see your doctor along with the reports (rather than visiting the doctor, conducting the blood test and going back for a follow-up). Find out if you need to come in a fasting state for any consultation.
3. *Minimize your contact with healthcare workers:* It is preferable to get your blood or urine tests from the same hospital setup rather than visiting a separate testing centre or asking for a home collection and then visiting your regular hospital for the OBG check-up. By this, you minimize the number of healthcare workers you will be coming in contact with.
4. *Trust your OBG and don't go seeking for second opinions:* There will always be a slight difference of opinion in the medical care being provided by two different doctors. Trust one and go with his/her advice. You will unnecessarily burden yourself with worry by seeking

multiple opinions. Overthinking will not just put you in a vicious cycle of second guessing your doctor but also expose you to multiple healthcare providers in search of the 'right opinion'.

What to Expect after Delivery

Just because social distancing is the norm these days does not mean a pregnant or postpartum woman needs to be totally isolated. We cannot sacrifice on the quality of care or support a woman needs around and after childbirth. If you need your mother to assist you, then please you should ask for it. The number of visitors and well-wishers coming to see your new baby can and should definitely wait. Mask or no mask, it is better to completely avoid courtesy visits.

As the epidemic marches on, and state borders are getting sealed every now and then, it might be difficult for your caregiver (mother/mother-in-law) to travel to your city. This should not dishearten you. You are capable of looking after yourself and the baby with the help of your partner. This epidemic sees more and more people continuing to work from home. The new father can ask for a parental leave. It is an extraordinary time we are living in. It is worth having the conversation with your manager regarding scope for a parental leave to lend support at home to the new mother.

Breastfeeding during the Pandemic

Breastfeeding is 100 per cent encouraged at this time. All of us are going hunting for the Holy Grail of the ultimate immunity boost in turmeric (*haldi*), garlic, ginger and *amla*. Our newborn babies with their untouched immune systems need all the antibodies they can get from the mother's milk. So don't hesitate to exclusively breastfeed your baby. In fact, antibodies to Covid-19 have been detected in the breast milk, so it is all the more important to exclusively breastfeed your baby if you unfortunately catch the virus. It is advisable to find a lactation consultant during your pregnancy itself and have the important conversation with her regarding what to expect in breastfeeding. *Don't hesitate to seek lactation consultation at any point in your breastfeeding journey*. You will save a ton of money (formulas are expensive) and also give yourself and your baby all the healthy nutrition you can by the *amrit* (elixir) that your milk is.

Trying for a Baby

If you have been trying to conceive naturally or by assisted reproduction techniques, then withhold it for now. The lockdown guidelines are changing every other week and it's best to wait till this storm passes. A planned precious pregnancy in these uncertain times is a big no. An assisted pregnancy needs a lot of monitoring and follow-ups. It is advisable to wait. One of my patients who is a diabetic wanted to go ahead with trying for a baby during the lockdown. I advised her against it. She would need close monitoring of her sugars during the pregnancy and there are foreseeable complications due to diabetes. She would require more frequent check-ups throughout her pregnancy and I just could not guarantee her that kind of care considering the unpredictability of the times we are in. My advice to her was to work on her wellness and sugar control during the lockdown period.

Unplanned Pregnancies

According to the UNFPA, there could be around 7 million unplanned pregnancies from March to December 2020 in India. If you have an unintended pregnancy and wish to terminate it (for medical, psychiatric or social reasons) then please get in touch with your doctor. *The Covid-19 pandemic should not be your reason to want to terminate your pregnancy.* There is no evidence of mother to child transmission of the virus during pregnancy or via breastfeeding as of now. Close contact between mother and child is inevitable and that itself would transmit the virus.

You must get a medical opinion first if you wish to terminate the pregnancy. Do not get abortion pills from your pharmacist and take them without a scan. Taking these pills without an ultrasound confirmation of a uterine pregnancy can be hazardous (abortion pills are not given in case of an ectopic pregnancy. An ultrasound is needed to confirm the location of the baby).

Supporting a Pregnant Friend during the Pandemic

If you have a friend or relative who is pregnant or has just delivered, then these are the things you can do to help her out while social distancing:

1. Do not visit her. Don't compel her to make the tough choice of asking you to not come. She is alone and wants all the reassuring presence of her friends. Keep yourself, her and the baby safe by maintaining the distance. Be available with kind words.
2. You could help her out with tasks which are simple and may take her time to do. Order groceries, diapers and supplies for her. Help her by finding a lactation consultant if she needs one. You will save her precious minutes of sleep by doing these simple favours.
3. Offer her a non-judgemental listening ear. Sometimes that's all a new mother needs. To be able to vent without being judged.
4. Do you plan to organize a socially distant baby shower for your friend? Order this book online and get it delivered to her address along with *ajwain* plant (it helps in respiratory infections, see page 112).

ACKNOWLEDGEMENTS

The instigation to write this book came just a day after my son was born in 2014. I had the smoothest pregnancy ever and just like any naïve new mother I had imagined delivery to be the worst. But the turn my life took after childbirth was a real jolt. My husband and I were overwhelmed by all the curveballs my postpartum threw our way. As he would desperately google our woes each day, we found ourselves more confused by the solutions that the internet had to offer. Clutching to each straw (medical guidance, opinions, free advice and home remedies), we somehow got by. As time passed, my postpartum problems were soon forgotten. But not being able to exclusively breastfeed was a personal defeat for me and that was something I couldn't let go of.

After my maternity leave of a year and a half, I rejoined my practice. As a doctor I looked at every new mother who walked into my office with a completely different lens. She was no longer a body having a medical problem. She was a woman affected by her child, her lack of sleep, her loss of identity and a lack of social support more than anything else. The more women I encouraged to share their emotional struggles, the more I found my treatment was not just limited to a prescription but an empathetic exchange between her (my patient) and me (the doctor). We were both mothers before anything else. Every time a tear was shed in my office, I got more determined to reach out to more new mothers and that's what gave birth to the concept of my book. I am grateful to every woman who shared her struggles with me. My patients who let me into their lives and bared their souls to me, I owe this book to all these brave women. I have heard and remembered all your stories while writing this book.

After my daughter was born and I was successful in exclusively breastfeeding her, did I gain the confidence to write this book, knowing well that all the challenges from my first postpartum had been conquered. Six months of writing later, I had a manuscript ready. Or so I thought. That's when I came in contact with my agent, Anish Chandy. One of the keenest eyes in the book business, he saw promise in my first proposal and almost signed me. Calling my original manuscript a 'glorified blog', he demanded of me a discipline (of a writing bootcamp) to churn out a book living up to the original vision with which I had pitched the book to him. Thank you for never accepting mediocrity in my work and eventually signing me.

My heartfelt thanks to my mentor, Dr Shaibya Saldanha, a wonderful gynaecologist, she has always insisted that every woman needs to be heard beyond her medical problems and taught me that no woman is just a medical diagnosis. There is always a backstory for why a woman suffers. How right you have been! I am also grateful to my other mentor, Dr Taha Mateen, for imbibing compassion in my medical practice in my formative years. You two continue to inspire me.

In the scheme of events, my brother, Farooq Adam was the toll booth I had to always revisit. At every milestone he has skillfully maneuvered my course to the finish line. You have been an intuitive guide and stopped me from making any wrong decisions. Also, he introduced me to Ambi Parameswaran who put me in touch with my agent. Thank you, Ambi Uncle, for hearing me out and giving your valuable feedback.

I have had the privilege to work with two wonderful editors. As a newbie in the writing world I had a perception that editors were rigid and capable of butchering a book. I couldn't be more wrong. You both have been very thoughtful and always helped with the edits without sacrificing the core values of my writing. Among the three of us, this book is already a bestseller as we have read and reread the manuscript hundreds of times! Priyanka Sarkar was my first editor before my book was signed by Pan Macmillan India. Thank you for teaching me the art of being succinct and simple. I am happy that our professional relationship has blossomed into a meaningful friendship. I'd like to thank my editor at Pan Macmillan India, Avneet Kaur, who has been a breeze to collaborate with. Thank you for letting me retain all my sarcasm and candidness in the book.

I want to thank my marketing advisor, Rajveer Singh Rathore, and my creative designer, Balaji Ganesan, for helping with my Facebook page, Instagram handle and YouTube channel, Momstein, to market my book. You two have been my buoy when I dived into the world of social media.

My book would not have been possible without all the remarkable women in my life. My heartfelt thanks to my sister-in-law, Asiya, who has been my pillar of strength and support ever since I married her brother. My friends, Nazia, Manu and Vibha for sharing their lives and having endless discussions with me on the challenges of motherhood. I have shared parts of this book with many more wonderful women. It is not possible for me to name everyone in this tiny acknowledgement. Your good wishes and support have kept me going the last three years.

My mother, who treated me no different from her sons and raised me to always only compete with myself. She has always told me, 'Once you set your mind to something, nothing can stop you.' *Mumma, I did set my mind to something and now it looks like a book.*

My mother-in-law and father-in-law. You never objected to my time-consuming–alternate career path and only encouraged me. Every time I locked myself in my study to write, not once did you make me feel uncomfortable for leaving the kids with you both. Despite being troubled by my little ones, you always made the atmosphere at home very positive. I am blessed to be your daughter-in-law.

My terrific children, Ahmad and Maria. Without all the troubles faced mothering you two, I would not have been able to write this book. But I wouldn't trade those troubles for the world. You give my life meaning and I am proud to be your mother.

The best husband in the world, Abdul Hadi. You motivate me, pick me up in times of self-doubt and nudge me to be a better version of myself. Especially during the Covid-19 lockdown you have wonderfully supported me by taking up potty-cleaning duty, setting the dinner table and discussing marketing strategies after our noisy bunch would fall asleep. You are a wonderful father and I am okay with our kids loving you more than their Mumma.

NOTES

Chapter 2: The New Mother's Diet

1. Liu. N., Mao,L, Sun, X. et al. *Post-partum practices of puerperal women and their influencing factors in three regions of Hubei, China.* BMC Public health 6, 274 (2006) doi:10.1186/1471-2458-6-274.

Chapter 3: Looking After the New Baby

1. Montagu, Ashley, *The Womb of Time,* Touching, Page 67, New York, Harper & Row, 1986.

2. Ferber MD, Richard, *Solve your child's sleep problems,* New York, Simon and Schuster, 2006.

Chapter 6: Body Image Issues

3. McClure, C.K., Catov, J., Ness, R. et al. *Maternal Visceral Adiposity by Consistency of Lactation.* Matern Child Health J 16, 316–21, 2012.